D0962013

STRAIGHT TALK FOR STARTUPS

100 Insider Rules for Beating the Odds—
from Mastering the Fundamentals to Selecting
Investors, Fundraising, Managing Boards, and
Achieving Liquidity

Randy Komisar and Jantoon Reigersman

HARPER
BUSINESS

An Imprint of HarperCollinsPublishers

STRAIGHT TALK FOR STARTUPS. Copyright © 2018 by Randy Komisar and Jantoon Reigersman. All rights reserved. Printed in the United States of America. No part of this book may be used or reproduced in any manner whatsoever without written permission except in the case of brief quotations embodied in critical articles and reviews. For information, address HarperCollins Publishers, 195 Broadway, New York, NY 10007.

HarperCollins books may be purchased for educational, business, or sales promotional use. For information, please email the Special Markets Department at SPsales@harpercollins.com.

FIRST EDITION

Designed by William Ruoto

Library of Congress Cataloging-in-Publication Data has been applied for.

ISBN 978-0-06-286906-7

18 19 20 21 22   LSC   10 9 8 7 6 5 4 3 2 1

For all the Rule Breakers who make this world a better and more interesting place.

In memory of Bill Campbell and Tom Perkins,
Rule Breakers Extraordinaire.

CONTENTS

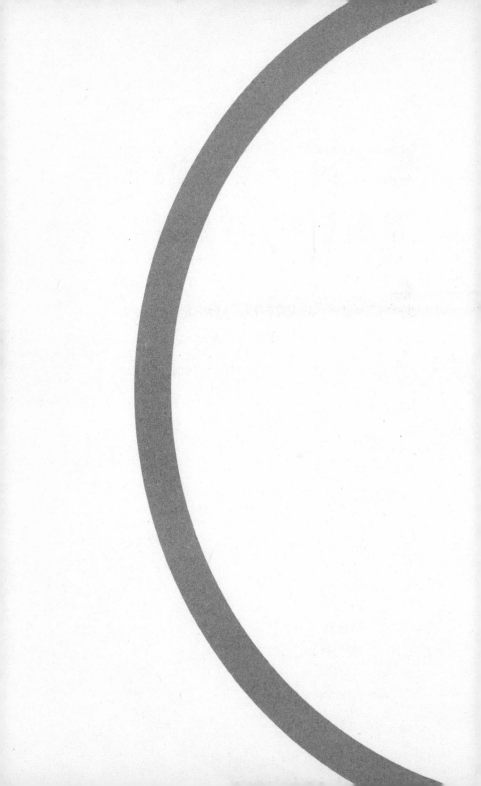

STRAIGHT TALK FOR STARTUPS

Part 5: Achieving Liquidity 219

INTRODUCTION

Y ou can't help but be impressed by the widespread enthusiasm for entrepreneurship today. What started as pockets of largely government-funded research and development in the United States following World War II has bloomed into a global economic phenomenon. Thirty years ago, entrepreneurs were a rare breed of iconoclast. The second wave of Silicon Valley (the first being semiconductor companies like Intel and National Semiconductor, thus the name Silicon Valley) was led by hippies in search of a personal technology utopia. Compared with today's sophisticated army of founders, equipped with glossy pitches and ambitions measured in billions, not just millions, those flower children were naïve, wide-eyed idealists.

And while Silicon Valley is still iconic, the entrepreneurial explosion is global: Stockholm, Berlin, Cambridge, London, Tel Aviv, Bangalore, Hyderabad, Beijing, Shanghai, and on and on. There is no monopoly on innovation. There is invention wherever there are smart people, and that is everywhere. Even the name Silicon Valley is a misnomer. What started in the orchards north of San Jose is now in full bloom up the Bay in San Francisco, as well as in Oakland. But entrepreneurship is more than mere invention; it is the best practice for creating market value from innovation, with limited resources. And while it is remarkable how quickly other places in the world are narrowing the gap between themselves and Silicon Valley, there is still an advantage to the incumbent.

Is it the venture capital? Yes, *but* . . . The *but* being that capital follows opportunity; it doesn't create it. As other places on the planet demonstrate monstrous financial successes like Baidu and Alibaba, Skype and Spotify, investors will follow.

Is it the attitude toward risk? Sort of . . . For more than seventy years, Silicon Valley has developed a constructive view of failure. Realizing that success is not within anyone's control—unless you failed for being dumb, lazy, or criminal—the Valley doesn't punish you for your business failures; to its great advantage, it puts your hard-earned experience back to work on the next big thing. Compare this with most other business cultures, where failure disqualifies you from future opportunities. Still, it is hard to argue that bold entrepreneurs in China, Israel, Sweden, and elsewhere aren't comfortable with the same daunting levels of risk.

Is it the experienced talent? Yes, *and* . . . The *and* being that it's not simply that the best talent comes to Silicon Valley from all over the world to seek their fortunes; it's that successful talent stays in Silicon Valley and reinvests itself in each new generation of entrepreneurs. While a successful European entrepreneur may make a hasty retreat to the South of France, in Silicon Valley the winners double down as angel investors, venture capitalists, board members, advisers, coaches, and mentors. If you walk into a Sand Hill Road venture capital office and see a gray-haired, lanky bloke in Birkenstocks sitting across the table from a young woman in jeans and an untucked shirt, chances are she is an entrepreneur getting a direct hit of wisdom from a mentor who has been down a similar path more than a few times before. He may already be wealthy enough not to care whether the meeting will turn into money, but he is intent on staying relevant by sharing hard-won lessons with a new generation of aspiring entrepreneurs.

Have you ever felt like everyone else knows something they just aren't telling you? That no matter how close you get to the source of money, talent, and wisdom, you can't quite get through the door? The ability to help entrepreneurs accelerate past this stage of confusion is the Silicon Valley advantage. It's not the big things; it's the little things—the wealth of experience, the tricks of the trade, the wisdom shared by the winners but somehow just out of the reach of the contenders.

That is why we wrote this book.

Collectively, we have been privileged enough to have front-row seats in this world for the past forty-five years. I have been a partner at the venerable venture capital firm Kleiner Perkins since 2005. I started as a lawyer and entrepreneur in Silicon Valley more than thirty years ago. I am a bit of a jack-of-all-trades—an entrepreneur, a seasoned CEO, and an investor all in one. My operating career spans decades, beginning with a private legal practice in technology law and then moving on to positions as senior counsel at Apple, co-founder and VP Business Affairs at Claris Corp., CFO and VP Operations at GO Corp., CEO of LucasArts Entertainment, and CEO of Crystal Dynamics. I have invested in and sat on the boards of dozens of innovative startups, like WebTV, TiVo, RPX, and Nest, as well as many social ventures. In the 1990s I created the role of "Virtual CEO," partnering with innovative founders to help them develop into leaders and turn their ideas into businesses. I also wrote *The Monk and the Riddle* and co-authored *Getting to Plan B* and *I F**king Love That Company*. For the better part of a decade, I taught entrepreneurship at Stanford University.

Jantoon first parachuted into his role as an executive of a Silicon Valley–backed venture almost a decade ago. He spent the earlier part of his career in mergers-and-acquisitions investment banking at Morgan Stanley and in special-situations investing roles at Goldman Sachs. He came to Silicon Valley with great admiration for its bold, boundless thinking. Soon, however, Jantoon realized that, while dreaming and innovating are fundamental to Silicon Valley's success, without excellent execution it is all for naught. He noticed that entrepreneurs were constantly reinventing the wheel, oblivious of the hard-learned lessons of their predecessors. Despite having access to a sophisticated board and several hundred millions of dollars of investment from many of the leading venture funds, strategic investors, and sovereign wealth funds, Jantoon experienced firsthand the failure of operating discipline that results from a lack of alignment between founders, management, investors, and the board.

We first met at a Kleiner Perkins event. When I discovered that in between jobs, Jantoon spent his time climbing twenty-thousand-plus-foot peaks and diving five hundred feet below the sea, we became fast friends. We would get together whenever Jantoon came to town, largely to catch up on his latest adventures, but inevitably our discussions returned to business. Specifically, to what really was going on in the Kabuki Theater of venture capital and startup boards. Jantoon thought he knew the rules, but at some point, the boardroom always seemed to tilt on him, and he was loath to believe that smart people could do such dumb things. He kept wondering what he was missing.

And so our chats became freewheeling romps, psychological analyses, and financial forensics. Jantoon caught on quickly and began seeing the light behind the shadows. As he understood more about the business of venture capital, the incentives for directors, and the magical investment math of the capitalization tables, things started to click.

Jantoon had also developed a close relationship with Tom Perkins, one of the pioneers of venture capital. This wasn't a surprise to me: Tom always loved freethinkers, adventurers, and iconoclasts. He is a legend in Silicon Valley. His career spanned entrepreneurship, senior management, and, most notably, venture capital. In 1972, Tom formed Kleiner Perkins Caufield and Byers with his co-founder, Eugene Kleiner. Their partnership and legacy have given life to some of the most significant and innovative businesses in the world: Google, Amazon, Nest, Intuit, Netscape, Sun Microsystems, Compaq, Tandem, Genentech, and many others. Tom became Jantoon's mentor, swapping his own stories about the inside workings of startups and venture capital.

In Tom's time, entrepreneurs and investors set out to grow businesses meant to last. The market's emphasis on the fundamentals of value gave them little choice. There were no quick exits. Tom had to build sustaining value by rolling up his sleeves and committing for the long haul; he locked arms with the entrepreneurs he invested in, roaming the halls of his portfolio startups and assisting directly in decision making and execution. He was an engaged and experienced partner to the founders.

Today, despite the startling levels of venture capital available, entrepreneurs aren't getting the hands-on help and guidance they need. Many board directors and investors lack any relevant operating or entrepreneurial experience, and they are content to play passive roles. These days, the financial industry gamut—from hedge funds, pension funds, and private equity firms to universities, family-run foundations, and foreign governments—are all chasing the same billion-dollar unicorns. Many venture capitalists are notorious for making absurd predictions and statements, especially through social media and the fanboy press, without ever being held accountable for outcomes. Erratic behavior among investors and directors confounds rational performance.

Entrepreneurship risks becoming just another fad, a lifestyle rather than a passion. When asked about their plans, so many young people answer that they want to be entrepreneurs without really understanding all that it entails. They have been sold a pitch of free food, unsupervised work, open offices, fun-loving camaraderie, and a chance at the gold ring. But being an entrepreneur is not just about living the life; it's about the hard work of bringing to life meaningful innovations and creating valuable businesses from them. Having an idea is not good enough; knowing how to make that idea a reality is what counts, and that is what this book is about.

There is a lot of attention paid to the many missteps of entrepreneurs, and with good reason. Their mistakes and transgressions don't affect just them; they affect the lives of millions relying on their innovations and can cost investors tens or hundreds of millions of dollars. If someone learns to drive in a beat-up Honda, the Honda will come back dinged. And if they learn to drive in a Ferrari, no one should be surprised if the Ferrari comes back dinged as well. But those dents are much more expensive and consequential, and there is far less tolerance for them. Entrepreneurs today don't have the luxury of learning by trial and error; they need all the help that experience and wisdom can bring, as fast as they can get it.

That's why we're offering straight talk for entrepreneurs in the pages that follow. Here we're sharing the "secrets" and rules of thumb we've gleaned from decades of being on both sides of the table—originally as entrepreneurs looking for advice and more recently as mentors trying to cut through the confusion on behalf of those who seek clarity. Consider this your playbook for understanding what venture capitalists and directors are really thinking so that you can be better partners with them. We hope to accelerate your learning, and save you from a few dinged doors along the way.

We cover a range of topics that every entrepreneur faces, especially in the early stages of launching their venture: planning and pitching, investors and board members, funding and liquidity, management and operations. While there are plenty of tomes on entrepreneurship, we have distilled our discussions and experience to the bare essentials: our 100 rules. You may know a little or a lot about a few of these topics, but unless you are a veteran entrepreneur, chances are you haven't yet pulled all the pieces together into a coherent game plan.

You must be fluent in all the issues facing entrepreneurs if you hope to win. This book will help you do that.

We refer to these insights throughout as "rules," but we are fully aware that there are no hard-and-fast rules that apply to every situation. Circumstances differ. Nevertheless, these entrepreneurial best practices have been burnished by experience and have survived the test of time. They aren't merely good pieces of advice; they are the prime directive. Learn them, understand them, bend them, and break them— but don't ignore them. They will get you through the sticky times and fortify you in the best of times.

This book is divided into five parts: Mastering the Fundamentals; Selecting the Right Investors; The Ideal Fundraise; Building and Managing Effective Boards; and Achieving Liquidity—the areas that we saw could readily be improved with some good old blocking and tackling. It draws from all three generations of our venture experience. Straight talk and the inside scoop—that's our mission in writing this book. Read it in any order and refer to it whenever you need the benefit of experience. Whether you are an entrepreneur, manager, investor, board director, or student of business, this is the playbook for anyone who ever wondered, What is really going on behind the curtain, and how can I take control and beat the odds?

MASTERING THE FUNDAMENTALS

The rules in part 1 address the fundamentals of preparing a startup business plan, obtaining the best funding, and engaging the most effective board members to help support the mission.

There are shelves of textbooks and manuals that purport to teach entrepreneurship. We instead focus our attention on just the essentials. The crucial things, like creating two financial plans, not one; hiring part-time experts rather than full-time trainees; knowing what to measure and the pitfalls of doing it too early; and the criticality of unit economics and working capital. There is a lot to know about startups, but we want to make sure you know a few key rules by heart.

And we cast a wide net: telling your story with your financials, practicing minimally invasive management, recruiting with the thoroughness of a preflight checklist, and taking advantage of disappointment, to name just a few of the topics. You may consider yourself a connoisseur of all things entrepreneurial and be an avid follower of the Twitter musings of smart investors and founders. Perhaps you are up to the second on who got funded and what new idea just launched. You may already have a deep understanding of one or more of the startup food groups—engineering, finance, operations, management, marketing, and sales. But unless you have been in the game a long while and are on a first-name basis with those tweet-lebrities, chances are you haven't had a chance to assemble a complete understanding of exactly what matters and what doesn't. In this section we pull from all the skill sets to provide you with a firm foundation for beating the odds.

RULE 1

Starting a venture has never been easier; succeeding has never been harder.

Whenever we hear this platitude recited for entrepreneurs, we see the faces of the wannabe founders light up. Unfortunately, while they are rejoicing at the ease of getting started, they seem to miss the second part entirely: it is really hard to succeed. It's a bit like learning a new language: you master "hello" and "goodbye" and then you have to face the arcane rules of grammar that stand between you and fluency. Easy to start, hard to succeed. This book is all about making the hard easier.

So why is it so easy to start something? First, venture capital is plentiful in the dominant hubs of innovation, especially Silicon Valley. This may reflect a wrinkle in time. Since the Great Recession of 2008, interest rates have been depressed worldwide. This means that hungry investors have had to stray into areas of risk usually reserved for experienced startup investors with plenty of intestinal fortitude. Sovereign funds, growth funds, private equity funds, and strategic corporate investors are chasing higher returns and ignoring the risk that accompanies them. And then there are the newly minted angel investors, individuals who find themselves with an excess of discretionary means, often because of their own entrepreneurial success, who become relatively casual funders of new ideas. These dynamics may present professional investors with reason to worry, but it's a positive development for entrepreneurs raising money. With a greater supply of capital from an array of sources, raising money is easier than ever, and deal terms favor the entrepreneur.

So why is it harder to succeed? More money brings more startups, which crowd markets with more competition hell-bent on rising above the crowd. That fuels irrational behaviors, such as "non-economic growth." Non-economic growth is when you price your product or service lower than the amount that the product or service contributes to the operating income of the business—for instance, when you sell ready-made meals delivered to the home for $10 while spending $5 on ingredients, $3 on preparation, $3 on packaging, and $5 on delivery. Most kids with a lemonade stand would see the folly of this business model. But the hope is that you can win more loyal customers faster than your competition while slowly lowering costs and raising prices. The problem is that once one company starts down this road, investing its venture capital in acquiring customers who are only coming for the free food, all the other competitors need to follow suit. Massive amounts of capital are wasted because one or more parties have raised a war chest that allows them to bleed red ink, at least for a while. Combine that with the fact that almost any new idea brings clones raising their own war chests and it's no surprise that the competitive landscape becomes crowded and non-economic.

Hiring, too, becomes more difficult and more expensive. Your employees act like free agents rather than comrades in arms, updating their LinkedIn profiles the day they start and ready to move to the competition at your slightest misstep. Real estate is scarce and dear. And the experienced mentors and directors who can help navigate all this, if you can get their attention, are stretched to the limit.

So while it's easy to get started, money and talent are spread thin by the proliferation of competition as investors gamble on trends over substance. But if you know the rules and understand everyone's motivations and peculiar self-interest, you may be able to win nevertheless.

RULE 2

Try to act normal.

There is nothing normal about being an entrepreneur. The norm is not to turn down or leave a well-paying job with benefits. Or to put your family and friends on hold for years while you devote every ounce of energy to an idea that others likely view with plenty of skepticism. It's not the norm to sleep on a futon under your desk, sipping energy drinks by the case and eating some god-awful synthetic food bars because there just is not enough time in the day to do everything that needs to be done. Or to look over your shoulder obsessively to make sure the competition isn't coming for you. And it certainly is not the norm to risk your career and livelihood on a dream and a prayer. Entrepreneurs need to believe, irrationally, that they are immune to the forces that defeat the normals every day and that they can succeed where a host of others have failed.

Venture capitalists have one of the greatest jobs in the world. They get to sit across the table from passionate strangers who hallucinate the future for them. These entrepreneurs tell investors about a future they haven't even imagined and how, with some money, talent, and a little luck, they can make it a reality. (Actually, they usually leave the *luck* part out, but we know better.) The investor then has the privilege of choosing which precious lunatics to join on their journey. Great entrepreneurs have a gleam in their eye and a chip on their shoulder. They can't contain themselves. If only you could dream the dream with them and dismiss the obvious obstacles to success. It's the lunatics who change the world, not the normals.

You might think, with all the fawning press and deafening hype insisting that everyone quit their day job and become an entrepreneur, that entrepreneurship is for everyone. If the classic movie *The Graduate* were made today, Dustin Hoffman's character would be advised to pursue startups, not plastics.

When meeting potential investors and comrades in arms, however, you must try to act normal. Don't let them know you are one of those precious lunatics hell-bent on changing the world until you've gotten to know them better. You don't want to scare them off right at the start.

Entrepreneurs are the exception, not the norm.

RULE 3

Aim for an order-of-magnitude improvement.

I f you are going to challenge the status quo, you have to give people a reason to change their behavior. The biggest challenge you face will be the inertia of your customers, who are prone to settling for "good enough." A successful new venture needs to bring at least a tenfold improvement to some aspect of a market or product; we call this the "order of magnitude" contribution factor. While ten times is the minimum, a hundred times obviously would be even better.

If you don't target at least an order-of-magnitude goal, you are unlikely to convince your investors and customers to take a chance on you. What has to be improved tenfold? That depends on your business. If your product is aimed at improving the performance of another product already on the market, try for an order-of-magnitude improvement to capture the customer's interest. If you hope to reduce price in order to dominate an existing market, have a plan to ultimately create an order-of-magnitude improvement in the customer value proposition. Remember: your customers don't know you from Adam, and they need a good reason to take the leap, just like your investors and employees. With the flurry of me-too and copycat ventures, this fundamental rule is too often overlooked. It's not easy to deliver a tenfold improvement, but if you can't, think again before entering a crowded market.

Another advantage of aiming for an order-of-magnitude improvement is that it provides a wide target rather than a narrow bull's-eye. If you try to thread the needle with an innovation that is just good enough, you may well miss it entirely. But if you shoot for an order-of-magnitude change, you may still be in the game even if you miss it by half.

RULE 4

Start small, but be ambitious.

T he most famous and impactful entrepreneurs all have bold ambitions. They envision their innovations driving global change and massive opportunities. But unless you are fortunate enough to have a Midas-level track record, you are most likely unable to assemble all the resources you will need to chase the entire dream at once. You will have to cut to fit and stage your success, systematically focusing your limited resources on proving out the "leaps of faith" (the core assumptions in your plan that must be correct for you to succeed) at each juncture, until you can demonstrate to your stakeholders that your business is firing on all cylinders and only requires more fuel to reach your destination.

If you were Reed Hastings in 1997, and you had a vision for transforming the home entertainment business by streaming videos created by your own studio to a global audience, would you have tried to sell that vision to investors in the face of a slow, low-quality Internet and dominant cable and broadcast content-distribution players like Comcast and NBC? Or would you have sharpened your focus and attacked a large but vulnerable link in the chain—Blockbuster, the retail distributor of DVDs—with your own novel subscription service? And when Blockbuster offered to acquire your company and make you wealthy, would you have sold? Or would you have moved toward a strategy of distributing the existing library of movies over the Internet as the speed and the quality of service improved?

Fourteen years later, in 2011, when Hastings finally decided to train all his attention on the big idea and make a clean break with his DVD subscription business—naming it Qwikster to distinguish it from his sweeping vision of online entertainment at Netflix—customers weren't ready, and he wisely backtracked. One step at a time. Ultimately, Netflix has been able to realize its vision with award-winning content that is heralded for starting a renaissance of quality home entertainment serving a massive, binge-watching global audience. It has taken many billions of dollars, money Hastings could not have hoped to raise for such an outlandish idea in 1997. But Netflix didn't rush ahead of the developing technology, the evolving customer behaviors, or the changing competitive landscape. Instead, it successfully conquered physical distribution, online distribution, content creation, and global expansion as each opportunity became ripe for the taking. Patience, focus, and tenacity paid off. Not to mention an exquisite sense of timing and maybe a little luck.

Even entrepreneurs fortunate enough to command the resources necessary to chase the big idea directly need to pace themselves, testing fundamental assumptions and removing risk methodically. Rushing leads to missteps, which can lead to wasted time and opportunity. In fact, entrepreneurs should always conduct early, low-cost tests of their ideas to ensure that they are on the right track and the contribution factor is real.

If you grow rapidly based upon your untested assumptions, you risk derailing your innovation while squandering your resources on premature commitments made in the wrong direction and with the wrong partners. Remove the white-hot risks before doubling down and chasing the dream.

RULE 5

Most failures result from poor execution, not unsuccessful innovation.

Plenty of people confuse luck for skill. We flatter ourselves and find cause where there is none. The difference between skill and chance boils down to repeatability. You need to demonstrate, to your own satisfaction and that of your stakeholders, that you have the ability to make it rain whenever you want to, not just when it is cloudy and dark. It's those operating talents, organizational abilities, and know-how that make you a medical doctor, not a witch doctor. We can name plenty of badly designed yachts with sloppy crews and incompetent captains that still arrived at port just because there was a fair wind and they knew how to use a rudder and fill the sails. They were very lucky to be in the right market environment, but it does not mean they were good leaders, managers, or innovators. Even turkeys can fly in a high wind, and broken clocks are correct twice a day.

Timing is critical. If you are right about the market but wrong about the timing, you will fail just the same. I know of a venture capitalist whose response to each new business idea was "I had that idea ten years ago." Well, great, but ten years ago you would have failed, because the market conditions for success were absent. Now is the only time that matters. Can you deliver your product today at the right price, with the essential features, in a market ready for the improvements complete with the distribution channels needed to meet the demand? If so, you are ready.

While Steve Jobs (this wouldn't be a book on startups if it didn't mention Mr. Jobs) was a prodigious oracle of market trends, an equally important but less appreciated strength was his uncanny ability to never ship a product before its time. When Jobs returned to Apple in 1997, one of the first things he did was kill the Newton project. Newton was John Sculley's bid to provide a handheld communicator with handwriting recognition and online connectivity. It had struggled for years, fighting the technology curve and falling short on both price and performance.

Realizing the mismatch of vision and capability, Jobs unceremoniously terminated the project. But he kept brilliant talent like Tony Fadell and his sidekick Matt Rogers (who later founded Nest together) working in the area, first targeting digital music with the iPod. The technology and content were ready for a portable music player, and he could dominate that market while continuing to innovate on the bigger idea of a ubiquitous portable connected device. It was a decade later that Apple introduced the iPhone, a quantum leap from the Newton. The technology and batteries were finally cost-effective, the market had been primed to carry their entertainment in their pocket, and, by adding a cellular radio and a clever touch interface, Jobs finally had what he needed to deliver on the promise of a connected online communicator.

Taking a page out of Apple's playbook, the execution plan

for a successful venture is quite simple, with just six significant stages of development. But simple plans can be hard to execute; they require the utmost discipline. It's easy to get carried away with your vision and race ahead, betting on your assumptions, but that will introduce risks you don't need. When your innovation proves challenging and the results are disappointing, these setbacks are not necessarily "failures" if you learn and quickly refine your approach. You haven't failed until you stop trying or run out of money. Ventures need to be patient through this trial-and-error validation period. This should be the most inexpensive and agile time for a startup. If you needlessly compound your risk by building the business before you prove out your leaps of faith, then you lower your chances for success. Follow these instructions closely:

Stage 1: Idea—develop your idea and assess its attractiveness

Stage 2: Technology—build the technology

Stage 3: Product—deliver the product

Stage 4: Market—demonstrate market demand

Stage 5: Economics—prove unit economics in real life

Stage 6: Scale—now, finally, grow your business

(A mnemonic shortcut: "IT Provides ME Success"—Idea, Technology, Product, Market, Economics, Scale.)

The creative process is essentially an execution process, not a eureka moment. As with writing a book, you struggle doing the work for some time, hitting your head on the wall without success. But then an insight or a new development allows you to break through that wall, and the rest is execution. You can systematically "innovate" and execute your business while minimizing mistakes and maximizing your chances for success. In other words, there is some method behind the madness of entrepreneurship.

Naturally, the competition sometimes gets so heated, and the market is so prone to a winner-take-all scenario (think social networks, or Internet search), that you have to hustle and take additional risks to achieve dominate scale. But that is not a damn-the-torpedoes moment of rashness; it's a calculated strategy for how to accelerate through the six stages of growth.

RULE 6

The best ideas originate with founders who are users.

In general, the best innovations come from people who personally value and use them. Steve Jobs and Steve Wozniak wanted to bring the magic of IBM mainframes into their homes and created Apple Computer to pioneer personal computing. Travis Kalanick could not get a cab at a presidential inauguration event, so he created an on-demand car service and called it Uber. Google's search engine was built by Larry Page and Sergey Brin at Stanford as they struggled to make sense of the exploding amount of information online. Facebook was initially created by Mark Zuckerberg for Harvard students like himself to "rate" their fellow classmates. Yvon Chouinard started Patagonia so he could produce ecologically sound products for himself and his merry band of climbers and surfers. Tony Fadell needed a reliable way to manage energy consumption at his mountain home and invented the Nest thermostat. Reed Hastings was furious about his late fees at Blockbuster and created Netflix. All of these entrepreneurs started with a deep understanding of the needs of the customer because they were target customers themselves. When the market responded to their innovations, they built powerful businesses from their ideas.

This is a basic difference between an inventor and an entrepreneur. An inventor creates some amazing breakthrough that captures the imagination. An entrepreneur innovates a product or service that moves beyond imagination to address a real customer need that presents an attractive market opportunity. And don't confuse an entrepreneur with a CEO. A CEO brings leadership, strategy, and operations to build a successful business from an attractive market opportunity. One person may well be effective at all three—inventor, entrepreneur, and CEO—but they are distinctly different roles and competencies.

So when your idea is ready for the masses, it's time to move on to stage 2, building your technology.

RULE 7

Don't scale your technology until it works.

I t is tempting to believe you have a technology that works before it's proven. After all, if you are a technical founder, you know exactly how to do it in your head—you just need the time to get it done. But not so fast. Unless you are working on a simple, incremental innovation using existing technologies (something that is unlikely to garner you an order-of-magnitude improvement), then you still have some critical things that need to be sorted out. Accelerating your business based upon what you know leaves you vulnerable to paying the ultimate price when the things you don't yet know prove you wrong.

Nontechnical founders are even more prone to this mistake. They rely on their technical people, who assure them that they can deliver, or will soon, and based on those assurances, these founders start to scale their organization before the technology is actually working. Now their headaches are compounded. They hire more people and spend more money, increasing their monthly burn rate (the amount of money you are losing each month) and shortening the time until their cash-out date (the date at which all your money will have been spent if you continue on your current course), all in a rush to support a product that is not ready, even if the market for it is. And with each day, week, month that the product is delayed, you are losing even more money than you were before you scaled. You forfeit the early-stage startup advantages of lead time, nimbleness, and efficiency.

Sure, by moving more methodically, you risk not being able to scale your organization quickly enough, if by some outside chance your product does come together on time. But unless competitors are breathing down your neck, the wisest move is to scale more slowly and prudently. History bears this out.

What we like to call "restrained urgency" is a better approach. It can take a long time to get the technology right: so prove the technology, and only then scale your organization. In other words, first demonstrate that the product works; second, prove that the market potential is there; and third, get the economics (especially your "unit economics," which is the amount of money each sale contributes to your operating profit) straight. Otherwise you might find yourself bleeding to death before the medics arrive.

RULE 8

Manage with maniacal focus.

Legend has it that when Steve Jobs was presented with one of the early PowerBooks from the assembly line by his proud team, the first thing he did was turn it over to examine the bottom. They were all quizzical as they watched him grimace. The entire machine was carved out of a beautiful block of aluminum, but the bottom cover was not from the same block and was a slightly different shade of silver. Steve raged, demanding that they stop the production line and scrap all the offending machines, which cost hundreds of thousands of dollars. His team pointed out that no one ever looked at the bottom and that they could correct it in a future run. But Steve wouldn't bow to reason. He was maniacal about his products.

Breakthrough products are most often created by small teams, with strong leaders who eliminate all nonessential features in order to excel at the critical ones. There is no democracy in product development. It requires a benevolent dictator (hopefully not a tyrant) who may listen but will impose their will when needed. And perfection is not rational; it's not a business trade-off. To produce insanely great products requires more than a little insanity. What successful ventures have in common is clarity of purpose and a focus on the customer value proposition.

When Tony Fadell and Matt Rogers created the Nest

thermostat, no detail was left to chance. It took two years and dozens of the best people working around the clock. It seemed at times to some that the wheels might come off the car as tempers flared and feathers were ruffled, all in pursuit of perfection. Sure the process was exhausting and depleting, but when the product shipped, to rave reviews for its beauty and ingenuity, the Nesters felt a level of pride and satisfaction that only maniacal focus could deliver.

RULE 9

Target fast-growing, dynamic markets.

M any entrepreneurs target existing, large markets, because
that is where the money is—or so it seems. But the typical
mature market has five to seven relevant competitors, of which
two generally capture more than 70 percent of the profits and
therefore can out-invest the others. The competitive barriers to
a new entrant are daunting. This is why an order-of-magnitude
innovation is so important: you will need an unfair advantage
to disrupt the status quo.

However, it is best to avoid biting off too much too soon.
Instead, target smaller, specialized, higher-margin entry markets where you can establish a foothold. Focus on becoming
the leader within a market segment poised for fast growth, and
expand from there. This is what Tesla's stated strategy boils
down to: don't start by going after the big car manufacturers with
mass-market vehicles; rather, provide the well-heeled luxury
market's early adopters interested in paying for groundbreaking
clean-energy electric vehicles with high-priced cars that barely
cover manufacturing costs. Then, as your technology and know-
how move down the cost curve and your brand becomes even
more coveted, enter larger but more competitive higher-volume
segments of the industry. Resist subsidizing mass-market cus-

tomers with your expensive venture capital before you are certain it will help you quickly reach profitable volumes.

This is a variation on the innovator's dilemma, wherein a market leader rejects introducing an innovation because its quality and/or price does not expand its existing large market. The incumbent's product is at the waning edge of the technology S curve of price, quality, and features. New entrants seize the opening to sell a suboptimal product (high price, limited features, and/or technology constraints) to an early-adopter market and expand their market as their functionality increases and cost decreases, ultimately toppling the incumbent.

When Sony entered the audio market with its transistor radio to compete against tube-powered hi-fi systems, it sold on price and convenience, not quality. What we are suggesting is that you actually find niche markets with deep enough pockets to pay for you to develop the full power of your innovation while you are still on the expensive side of the S curve. Then expand your market later as costs fall and functionality continues to improve. The original Tesla Roadster cost $109,000 and had a range of 244 miles. Nine years later, the Tesla Model 3 costs $35,000 and has a range of 310 miles. Detroit, Munich, and Toyota City, beware.

Whenever Tom Perkins was asked about how venture capitalists would evaluate an idea or business plan, he would always answer with a joke: "I cannot tell you how to write or create one; I can only tell you how we read one: we start at the back, and if the numbers are big, we look at the front to see what kind of business this is. It is not very sophisticated." Good advice: paint a big picture, but focus like a laser on the near-term business opportunity.

RULE 10

Never hire the second best.

Your startup's DNA is established in the early stages of its life. While every employee's experience and skills are paramount, each new hire also contributes to your company's culture, so be mindful of their character and the values that they bring. Your employees, in time, will screen and interview additional candidates, and their biases will be multiplied throughout your organization. It is said that A players are confident enough to identify and hire A players, while B players hire C players. Mistakes in early hiring hurt.

While many companies find it trendy to write mission statements early in their formation, the complexion of your company actually takes form organically with each new hire. More time is spent wordsmithing these platitudes than actually instilling their essence into the organization. They may sit framed on everyone's desk, but mission statements are meaningless if they are easily ignored in everyday practice. It is advisable to wait until your core team is in place and has ample time to work together before setting in stone what you stand for and what you value. In the interim, simply clarify the qualities you would like to see in your organization and direct your recruiting against those.

Recruiting may seem like an exercise in filling seats, but

for a startup, the process is much more complicated. Sure, you need the best product manager or lead engineer or controller you can find—and the sooner the better. But startup organizations are highly dynamic and constantly evolving, and your team should be capable of evolving, too, while navigating uncertainty and learning on the job, all with limited resources. The skills required for a successful career in a traditional Fortune 500 company are not identical to the skills needed for your startup. In fact, they may be counterproductive, because employees of big companies are skilled at managing organizational processes and politics and expect ample resources, all of which you need to keep to a minimum in a fast-moving company.

Moreover, the formal organization (leadership, management, board, teams) will regularly change at the different stages of the venture's life cycle. The objective is to find people with high ambition, raw intelligence, grit, comfort with uncertainty, a strong work ethic, and low ego—people who can get the job done and develop and take on more responsibilities down the road. Gut check each person in your organization regularly as to whether you see them doing that job in six months or a year. Anticipate how each person will need to grow in order to keep up with your business, and help them get there or plan for their transition.

Recruits to startups too often fixate on evaluating a specific role in the company when in fact they should understand that the role is just the entrée into the organization. Instead they should consider the opportunities for learning and advancement—

and, yes, financial gain—that the venture can offer them over time.

And remember that the least expensive, top-performing recruit to your company is the one you already have. You don't have to spend the time and money recruiting replacements if you can keep your best people happy and committed. You are recruiting employees from other companies, and they are recruiting from you. They don't want your average employees; they want your best. It's a lot less time-consuming and risky to invest in your proven performers than to recruit an untested new hire. Always know which of your people are in your top 25 percent. Make them understand how important they are to you. Surprise them with raises and spot performance bonuses. Refresh their stock options before their grants are fully vested. Look for opportunities to reward them with more challenges and responsibilities. Some companies wait for their people to come to them with other employment offers before they mobilize and counteroffer. This is a foolish practice. If your people know they need a job offer in order to receive a raise, they will answer those recruiting cold calls and get those offers. And even if they would have been completely satisfied working for you, once they have made the emotional break to look outside, you are risking their loyalty and commitment. You want to be proactive so that your best people can rest assured that you fully value them and that they don't have to always be looking for greener pastures.

A great startup team is constantly challenging conventional wisdom and pursuing potential that larger companies either cannot see or deem too risky. You will require an agile, committed organization if you are to outperform the competition. Many of the roles you will need to fill in the future aren't even defined yet. So favor hiring talented business athletes over specialists with deep experience, and whatever you do, be sure to retain your best people.

RULE 11

_____

Conduct your hiring interviews as if you were an airline pilot.

A irline pilots are meticulous in conducting their preflight cockpit checks. Some time ago, the aviation industry figured out that many accidents were the result of overlooking routine precautions and instrument settings. Pilots were being trained for extraordinary events and were ignoring the mundane. The solution was the Pre-Flight Checklist, a prosaic set of rituals that ensures no one is overlooking the obvious. Hospitals have more recently adopted similar checklists for things like surgeries, to remove the avoidable risks that can cause big problems. Many doctors trained in the state of the art recoil at such systematic processes, but the improved results are undeniable.

Like other aspects of entrepreneurship, recruitment also benefits from a more systematic approach. Because we spend our lives meeting new people and evaluating them, we think we can bring the same casual approach to recruiting. But if every interviewer is asking their own idiosyncratic variety of questions and focusing on random qualifications, how can your organization hope to hire the best people? Too often, managers and board members have not been sufficiently trained to conduct effective hiring interviews—resulting in vague, open-ended questions that reflect personal biases rather than objective priorities. These unconscious biases can result in your failing to identify the best talent with backgrounds different from your own, which compounds the risk that your startup won't attract the most talented people for the job.

That's why we recommend developing common criteria and a shared checklist that reflects the organization's needs and values. Use of a checklist and some consistency across interviews doesn't mean the process has to be dull—you can make the interview process as creative and free-form as you wish, so long as you know what you're looking for and your criteria are shared by others. Having many conversations with candidates is wise, but a hodgepodge of random opinions and inconsistent filtering mechanisms won't serve the organization well.

A part-time game changer is preferable to a full-time seat filler.

A startup is stretched for resources, particularly for money. Competing for talent is difficult when established businesses can afford to outbid you. You will often find candidates who could make a huge difference to your success, but you cannot afford them and they won't be swayed by your uncertain upside. What do you do? Do you settle for hiring the best you can while forfeiting the game changers?

The game changers are those people who can single-handedly reduce your white-hot risks. Who bring the missing ingredient to solving your engineering quandary or the brilliant solution to your marketing bottleneck. They are also the people who inspire others to deliver more together than they could separately. They offer the ideal combination of experience and the ability to address your splitting headache. It may be their résumé, their references, or their specific experience, but there is something about these people that suggests they won't be just another individual contributor or middle manager.

Sometimes it is essential that the role be filled by the best person who can give you their all, 24/7. Some things just need to get done. But other times you might find that bringing on a game changer part-time and augmenting that person with a junior staffer who can leverage their experience and judgment is both preferable and feasible. Some of these talented game changers may want a more flexible career or are between commitments. If you can structure the role to accommodate them and then extract as much of their know-how as possible, it can be a win-win.

Your finance organization is a good place to start. The purpose of the finance function is to inform and discipline operating performance by providing timely, useful financial and operational information and insights throughout the organization. If your finance organization does not provide that support, you need to make changes. Founders often make the mistake of believing that, while they need to hire very experienced software engineers for development, and the best experts in marketing and sales, they can get away with lesser mortals in finance.

There are two key parts to finance: financial reporting (aka "accounting and controls," which focuses on how your firm has performed in the immediate past) and planning (also called forecasting, planning, and analysis, or FP&A, which focuses on where your venture wants to head and tracking how to get there). You may think that because you are not pulling in revenues yet, you can go the cheap route in staffing finance, since it is just cost accounting. But it's the FP&A function that can help you most in the early days of the company. These are the people who will model your business and test your assumptions. They strongly influence your strategy through numbers and analysis. Their work serves as the touchstone for your critical strategic decisions. They are also key to creating the business plans that will raise you the money to continue.

You don't have to hire the most expensive finance person to do all of this—there are lots of experienced finance folks who can help on a part-time basis, and your board can assist you in finding them. Some Silicon Valley recruitment firms specialize in outsourcing higher-level finance talent for part-time roles. In other markets, you can draw on recently retired experts and experienced people who are seeking more flexible workplaces such as yours.

This approach doesn't apply only to finance. There are recruiting firms today that specialize in identifying such talent for a host of roles. You may not be ready for a full-time marketing executive, but rather than bring on a junior person to fill the gap, consider finding a strong marketing lead who is willing to work part-time for you to solve the complicated issues that only experience can. And even though you don't yet have meaningful sales, consider hiring a part-time, proven sales executive to plan and set up what you will need to rapidly expand later. Don't skimp: you want the best thinkers, so be creative.

RULE 13

Manage your team like a jazz band.

Jazz perfectly encapsulates the ideal collaboration you want in a startup team. With its emphasis on individual virtuosity, improvisation, and dynamism, a jazz ensemble depends on every member's ability to embrace risk, regardless of the instrument they play. Every player is part of a team in intimate conversation with one another, note for note; everyone has to stand out *and* blend in, pulling their own weight as individuals while taking cues from the other members about new opportunities to contribute. Without each other, there is no music. When playing, there is no boss, but rather a leader who brings out the best in everyone to achieve the perfect harmony. Each player knows that his solo must fit within the context of the whole, while they are free to improvise upon a theme. They have their arms open to the unknown, but they do not let go of their shared vision.

As in a jazz band, the leader of a startup is responsible for establishing a coherent strategy and set of priorities while empowering each member of the team to be creative and productive. You want minimally invasive managers who understand that their job is to get the most creativity and productivity out of their people, not to be the boss for the sake of being the boss. After all, your employees are not simply the means of production; they are your means of creation. Leaders need to be of service to those doing the creation and provide the environment for them to flourish. Think Miles Davis, Bill Evans, John Coltrane, Cannonball Adderley, Paul Chambers, and Jimmy Cobb.

In a business full of risk, too many egos—too many soloists who ignore the song's melody—are a liability. It is your job to help the entire band play their hearts out.

RULE 14

Instead of a free lunch, provide meaningful work.

Startups think they need to provide free lunches because industry leaders like Google and Facebook do. Of course, when you have nearly infinite gross margins in a highly leveraged, globally scaled business, you can afford to shower your people with perks. Just remember that plenty of other leaders, like Apple and Amazon, don't.

There always comes a time when the controller walks into the CEO's office and points out that free lunches are costing the equivalent of a new engineer. Then, as the company grows, lunch is not just the cost of another engineer but also a product marketing manager, and so on. All of this seems manageable when you ignore your shrinking cash account in anticipation of your next infusion of capital. But if the market shifts and capital is more costly or, worse yet, unavailable, you will have hard decisions to make. Those meals will quickly look expensive.

As everyone knows, clawing back perks, especially at a challenging time, is costly to morale. It's exactly the wrong moment to start being frugal. So be careful when you first decide to provide free perks like food or discretionary time, and consider how these things may complicate your future. If you think you are going to build a startup team by competing with Google on perks, you are sorely mistaken. The people you want will trade free lunches for meaningful work and career growth in a venture set on changing the world. The upside in experience, creativity, opportunity, and maybe even a financial payday down the line should matter more to the right candidates than free food. Purpose matters more than perks. Focus your energy and resources on what matters most.

RULE 15

Teams of professionals with a common mission make the most attractive investments.

Your investors need to feel they can trust you with their money. But they also need to feel inspired by a common vision and mission. Good investors will walk around your office and talk to employees and advisers as part of their due diligence efforts, often in informal settings. It is very easy to see discrepancies between what the leaders say and what the team is doing. This does not mean everyone needs to "dress up" for the occasion, which could rattle smart investors as well. But it does mean that the team should come across as a united tribe, aligned by a clear and common vision.

The same applies to outside advisers used in the fundraising process. Make sure you have respected and capable outside legal counsel, because they will play a critical role in keeping the process on track. If you enter the negotiations with weak advisers, your investors may get the wrong impression about your professionalism.

Your investors want to know that everyone on your side is for real—experienced, knowledgeable, or able to get expertise when necessary. Not only does that increase trust and the chances of getting funded, but it will save your investors and you from headaches later. Plus, your investors want to be sure that you recognize what you don't know and are able to get help when you need it. It's a red flag when you show up with a B team or with no one at all, suggesting that you are either too ignorant or too arrogant to realize you need more professionals on board.

Professionalism is paramount, but that doesn't mean you can squeak by without also giving your investors the chance to be part of a business they'll be proud of. They want to make money, for sure, but they want to join you in building something great, too. In other words, professionalism is essential, but it's not enough. Big dreams and an inspiring mission matter as well.

RULE 16

Use your financials to tell your story.

Financial reports and metrics provide a trove of invaluable information about your business and your company. Behind the numbers is a stream of insights about your team and your opportunity, and good investors make a living reading that river. The cash flow statement not only tells you how much cash the business is making, or not, and whether the venture has enough money for debt servicing and other payments, but it also shows you how the company is proportioning its resources (for instance, more in engineering and less in marketing) and prioritizing its efforts (e.g., more on large customers, less on smaller ones). It can pinpoint discrepancies in what the company says about itself—*We are growing astronomically!*—and what is actually happening: the company is paying large sums to acquire customers who appear to be off-strategy or uneconomic. It highlights false economies—such as when you are limiting headcount but increasing the spend on contractors. It raises questions about key indicators—are you, for example, slowly moving customer acquisition costs to the brand marketing category in order to meet your acquisition cost goals? It can reveal critical concerns about your strategy, such as the fact that emphasizing annual subscriptions over monthly subscriptions may bring in more deferred cash but requires longer amortization, resulting in lower reported revenue. Show us your budget and we can tell you your strategy.

The income statement provides information on how much customers are willing to pay for your product or service, the unit costs of production, and the resulting margins, as well as the associated overhead expenses. The balance sheet provides a vivid picture of the assets and liabilities of the company. And underlying all of this are a host of assumptions that, for an early-stage venture, are much more important than the forecasts themselves. As always, the power is in asking the right questions and challenging the right assumptions, rather than getting specific answers.

Ventures do not run out of cash overnight. If you can read the river, you will pick up on the warning signs. The best practice for early-stage ventures is to focus on cash burn from both an operational point of view—where the money is going—and a variance point of view: how your cash spending is different from what you had planned or anticipated. Over time, the trends in each reveal where you and your team need to focus and improve. They also raise strategic questions about whether you are on the right course. The feedback loop provided by the financials is invaluable in course correcting and refining all aspects of your business. Don't just post the numbers each month; scrutinize them for clues on how to improve your business.

RULE 17

Create two business plans: an execution plan and an aspirational plan.

Entrepreneurs seem to feel that when they present their business to investors or other stakeholders, they need to have a single, bulletproof financial plan.

They are half right. Ideally, you should establish two different financial plans. The first is an execution plan that the team believes it can achieve, with 90 percent certainty, given what they know or can foresee today. This plan determines the company's spending. Think of it as a bottom-up plan, where it is your job to fill in the top. Given that this is the execution plan, the certainty of attaining it should be high, and therefore the expenses should be forecastable.

The second plan is one of less certainty, perhaps 50 percent, but this one articulates aspirational growth that is aggressive yet still attainable with a stretch and some luck. It anticipates things you don't know yet and can't see, but upon which your ultimate business strategy depends. This is the top-down plan, where you need to fill in the bottom. This is not a fantasy plan, but rather one that, if some favorable events beyond your control come to pass, you can accomplish with hard work and diligent execution. This is the plan to use for aggressive top-line target setting, like performance compensation.

Separating the two plans and clearly articulating the elements necessary for achieving success are important in order to avoid overspending on an aspirational plan. For instance, too often management teams announce that they have missed their revenue target or their gross margin target yet attained their hiring target. That is a big problem, because this means they have missed their cash inflow while simultaneously increasing their overhead costs—a double whammy for the business. Or perhaps they are meeting their budget but behind in hiring, which means they are overspending on other things and will exceed their budget when they complete their hiring.

Stick to your execution plan until you have achieved the key milestones of your aspirational plan that give you the confidence to throw more wood on the fire. Be prudent and increase your spending incrementally, only as those milestones are achieved.

As an early-stage company, you will need to update these plans about every ninety days, effectively creating a rolling forecast rather than an annual plan. This means that every ninety days you are reforecasting the following four quarters. Things happen so quickly in a startup that the annual planning cycle is too slow and inaccurate. Last quarter's numbers quickly become out of date. Don't toss your operating and forecasting discipline out the window; simply establish a reality check every ninety days as you gain a better view of the future. And this rolling forecast is not an excuse to miss your numbers. Keep close track of your Annual Operating Plan (twelve-month plan), Quarterly Forecast updates, and Actual performance. Deviations provide you with important information about your business plan assumptions and the realities of your business. Every change should be fully documented and supported by facts. This process helps avoid the temptation to use overly optimistic, forward-looking cost-down curves and forecasts as a remedy for missed targets. Stay optimistic, but be sober.

And while predicting the future for an early-stage company is a bit like palm reading, you should create plans that extend out at least three years. Not that any three-year forecast is reliable at this point, but it forces you to contemplate the investments you need to make today to achieve your aspirations tomorrow. We have seen many ventures discover too late that their top-line revenue and gross margin ambitions are unachievable because they didn't hire the people or buy the equipment last year required to achieve this year's goals.

_____

*Know your financial numbers and their interdependencies
by heart.*

Like most everything else when it comes to starting a venture,
the financial mechanisms and metrics underlying your best-
laid plans are both art and science. It's the interplay between
the various elements that makes building a startup a matter
of both skill and sensibility. Nothing occurs in a vacuum—
especially when it comes to financial reporting. As in a finely
tuned machine, all the levers and pulleys must work together
to accurately gauge the health of your business.

Have you ever inserted a formula in a spreadsheet, just
to have it spit back that your calculation can't be completed
because it's a circular reference, meaning that the value of one
variable is dependent on the value of another variable that,
in turn, is dependent on the value of the first variable? The
income statement and balance sheet are that, in spades. You
need to understand those formulas, not just the calculated
results, if you are to get the most from your financial reporting.
How the numbers are calculated is only part math; the rest is
judgment—the best judgment of your financial team.

Here is a quick primer on how your financial numbers
work together:

INCOME STATEMENT

Sales

-   *Cost of goods sold*
- =   Gross profit (driver: margin)
-   *Operating expenses (drivers: margin, inflation)*
- =   EBIT (earnings before interest and taxes)
-   *Interest*
- =   EBT (earnings before taxes)
-   *Tax*
- =   Net income

CASH FLOW STATEMENT

Net Income

- +   *Depreciation*
- =   Operating cash flow
-   *Investment in working capital*
-   *Capital expenditures*
- =   Free cash flow
- +/-   *Change in debt*
-   *Dividend payments*
- +/-   *Change in equity*
- =   Change in cash

BALANCE SHEET

Assets

+ *Cash*

+ *Inventory*

+ *Accounts receivable*

+ *Plant/property and equipment*

= Total assets

Liabilities

+ *Accounts payable*

+ *Debt*

+ *Shareholders' equity*

= Total liabilities and shareholders' equity

WORKING CAPITAL SCHEDULE

+ *Change in inventory (driver: turns/sales)*

+ *Change in accounts receivable (driver: days sales outstanding)*

− *Change in accounts payable (driver: days outstanding/cost of goods)*

= Investment in working capital

DEBT AND CASH SCHEDULE

Beginning cash balance

+/− Change in cash

Ending cash balance (calculate interest income on average)

Beginning debt balance

+/− Debt pay-down/increase

Ending debt balance (calculate interest expense on average)

Note some of the most obvious interdependencies among the various reporting numbers. Interest is a key factor in determining EBIT and also a key factor on the debt and cash schedule ending balances. Net income from the income statement finds its way into the calculation of shareholders' equity in the balance sheet, as do dividend payments and changes in equity from the cash flow statement. Depreciation and capital expenditures are crucial elements of the plant/property and equipment line in the balance sheet. Investment in working capital in the cash flow statement is taken directly from the working capital schedule. The change-in-debt line in the cash flow statement is the result of the debt and cash schedule calculation, while the change-in-equity line comes from the balance sheet. And the balance sheet relies on the change in inventory, change in accounts receivable, and change in accounts payable calculated in the working capital schedule.

Now add another bit of complexity. All of these numbers require classification and tabulation by your finance team. They are more subjective than some would like to believe. That's where science meets art and sound judgment. Do you include total revenues shared with large vendors in your sales numbers, or do you net out the split before reporting just your slice? Your gross margins will change a lot based upon whether you use the gross or net denominator. Do you include trade discounts in your marketing expenses, or do you decrease sales to account for them? (This is often referred to as being "above" or "below" the line.) Are your property, plant, and equipment costs included in general and administrative expenses, or do you allocate them by headcount across all of your functional expenses? Do your contracts call for continuing services that don't allow you to realize the up-front payment as sales when received? Or are they de minimis and included as warranty expenses in your cost of goods? And does your lifetime subscription offering require you to realize revenues over an indeterminate number of years as you try to figure out what the lifetime of your customers is, significantly reducing your reported revenues in the current period?

You owe it to your financial team and your stakeholders to be able to drill down into the components of each element so you understand, for instance, why revenues have increased rapidly (more customers) but your operating margins have shrunk (discounts to accelerate sales, customers not as profitable as expected, etc.). Question how your sales and expenses are categorized and what those decisions mean for your business. Don't treat your numbers like obligatory mile markers; dig in and master them.

The numbers don't lie, but if you treat them as just that—numbers on a page—you're missing out on a big piece of your job as an entrepreneur. If you do dig deeper, you'll find that the numbers reveal the underlying narrative of your business, your priorities, your trigger points. They will help you crystallize a point of view on where the business has been and where it is going. And then you'll be able to share the plot with your employees, your investors, and other stakeholders—even if the final scene has yet to be written.

RULE 19

Net income is an opinion, but cash flow is a fact.

When there is a discrepancy between net income and cash flow, it may be for either of two main reasons. First, the income statement is updated with any sales made or revenues earned as soon as the transaction is completed. However, payments for such sales may actually be received much later, increasing receivables rather than cash. So even though the net income reflects earnings and the entrepreneur has made money in accounting terms, it is not yet available as cash flow and cannot be spent.

This is why too much growth can actually cripple your business in situations where the income statement and accounts receivable grow much faster than the cash flow available at any particular point in time. Such an imbalance in the net income and cash flow means that even though you are generating paper profits from your business, you still don't have enough cash to support expanding labor and materials.

Consequently, understanding your working capital is very important. Working capital is defined as the difference between current assets and liabilities. If you pay your vendors in thirty days and get paid in ninety days, you have to find at least sixty days of cash available from somewhere in order to take the order. This is referred to as positive operating working capital. If you want to grow quickly and increase your orders twofold each period, you will need to double that amount. On the other hand, if you get paid in thirty days but pay your vendors in ninety days, then each sale actually provides you with more cash to fuel faster growth. You are in effect "borrowing" from your vendors to invest in growth. This alchemy is called negative operating working capital, and it is the way Amazon's cash flows worked when it started out in the book business. So your capital-raising strategy and sources of capital depend heavily on how your cash flows work. From the very start, you should understand what your specific business model will require and plan your fundraising accordingly.

Second, net income or profit is a relatively arbitrary figure obtained after assuming certain accounting hypotheses regarding expenses and revenues. Cash flow, on the other hand, is an objective measure, a unique figure that is not subject to any personal criterion or discretion. Too many early startups with chief financial officers who have too much time on their hands report GAAP (generally accepted accounting principles) calculations of revenues and gross margins rather than cash flow. This obscures the implications of working capital and receivables timing. Cash is king, so count it, at least twice a day. For early-stage startups cash should be all that matters.

Unit economics tell you whether you have a business.

I f you plan to build a real business, gross margins and profit margins are critical. Ideally, both need to be sustainable over time. If you make a dollar, you are in control, but if you lose a dollar, your investors and creditors call the shots.

Unit economics is a simple concept. For every discrete sale of your product or service, do you make money? This is before considering all the operating costs of your business. If your product costs you $2 and you sell it for $1, your unit economics are negative $1. If you sell it for $3, your unit economics are positive $1. What you are aiming for is positive unit economics, resulting in a positive contribution margin, the amount each sale contributes toward paying your operating expenses, like your engineers and marketing folks. If you have positive unit economics and you are able to scale your business with leverage—meaning that you don't have to incur an additional $1 of operating expenses for each additional $1 of contribution margin—then you are on your way to building a real business.

Revenues without positive margins are just expenses. When evaluating margins or unit economics in ventures, management often focuses on a single-user case. Their plan highlights one type of customer, in one channel, with one need. Don't mistake this for a true market analysis; this just means you can sell one product, once, to a very specific customer. Make sure not to fool yourself. Test your unit economics assumptions across a wide range of product applications and real-life customers and markets. Include all fully loaded costs: transportation, warranties, financing costs, and so on. When you leave something out, you skew your results and prioritize the wrong things internally.

In practice, figuring out unit economics is complex and dynamic. It is therefore important to create a robust unit economics framework so that as input costs change over time, you can continue to update the model. Understating how the unit economics vary across markets, customer applications, and geographies is paramount to setting your strategy. Averages can be misleading.

When unit economics don't support your strategy, it is a common mistake to explain away the problem by forecasting lower future costs as you move down the production cost curve. Most often this is just wishful thinking. There are certainly businesses that require threshold volumes to provide favorable pricing and amortization. You should know exactly what those volumes are and how much capital you will need to invest in unprofitable growth so you can achieve those threshold volumes and make the business work. It is fine to invest in near-term uneconomic growth if you are highly confident that you have the capital to fund achieving profitable scale; however, fully understand all your assumptions and appreciate the risk you are taking.

Confusion often arises in differentiating volume-driven unit economics from technology-driven unit economics. The former operates on well-understood production cost-down curves: the charts that show declining product costs as volumes increase because of efficiencies in labor, volume discounts on components, improved designs that reduce parts, better amortization of facilities, etc. Technology-driven unit economics are very different, however, relying on uncertain advances in technology to drive down expenses. While there may be a rational approach to investing capital to achieve volume economics, the better approach for technology-driven economics is to target higher-value, less cost-sensitive niche markets and expand as the maturing technology lowers your costs.

For instance, solar cells were initially limited in their efficiency by materials science. They were, however, still valuable to very high-end markets, like facilities in remote locations where other sources of power were prohibitively expensive. Targeting those customers as you continue to experiment with the materials to dramatically increase efficiency and then broaden your market is a better strategy than forward-pricing your existing inefficient chips to be attractive to today's market and losing money while you pray for a technology breakthrough.

Foolish assumptions about how you'll be able to drive down volume costs sink many businesses. Make sure you're not giving away money with every product sold; that is a losing proposition no matter what. Sure, giving away razors can be a good business, but only after you are confident that customers will buy enough blades to provide positive combined-unit economics. Nobody has ever made up for negative unit economics by shipping in volume. Be disciplined or the market will discipline you. Bleeding capital on every sale is no joke. While competition may force your hand, scaling too quickly is often driven by un-realistic assumptions about your real unit economics as much as it is by impatience and hubris. If you know your true unit economics you can build a strategy to compete without spending your way to failure.

Manage working capital as if it were your only source of funds.

Effectively employing working capital—the difference between current assets and current liabilities—is the Holy Grail for funding early-stage companies. Whether negative or positive, it indicates not only the company's ability to meet its short-term financial obligations but also its ability to truly "sweat" its short-term assets. Management of working capital involves inventory management and the mastery of accounts receivable and accounts payable, including consideration of short-term debt service. Remember to be laser-focused on the working capital ratio (current assets divided by current liabilities), the collection ratio (a company's average collection period ratio is a principal measure of how efficiently it manages its accounts receivable), and the inventory turnover ratio (cost of goods sold divided by the average inventory for the period, which reveals how rapidly a company's inventory is being sold and replenished).

Let's dissect these for a moment. The working capital ratio is a good indicator of how much cash is available for growth. When the ratio shrinks, you have less cash to meet your short-term needs. When it expands, you can invest more in growth. Mind you, if you are collecting from customers faster than you are paying vendors, your operating working capital ratio may be a fraction rather than a multiple, but that can actually be a benefit to funding a fast-growing business. Know the range in which your business model is comfortable and react quickly if you fall below the minimum. The collection ratio lets you know how quickly you are getting paid, as well as when your customers are stiffing you. Keep close track of the "days sales outstanding" (DSO): this number will signal when you are booking un-economic customers and will also be an early warning of stresses in your target market. Manage it like a hawk. "Inventory turn-over" may seem like a quaint phrase in the era of digital products and services, but it is still hugely important. If you have to keep finished products in warehouses before shipping, or parts in bins before production, this will tie up precious capital and significantly impact your business growth and success. A simple change like taking ownership of inventory at the destination point rather than the shipping point can mean sizable sums to a company whose goods are shipped by boat from overseas. And inventories that grow as fast or faster than shipments point to sales challenges—like excessive returns or poor channel sell-through—that need to be addressed immediately. The more frequently your inventory turns over—i.e., is sold and replaced by new inventory—the healthier your bottom line.

Growing businesses require cash, and being able to free up cash by shortening the working capital cycle, reducing DSO, and increasing inventory turns is the least expensive way to grow, if you can do it. Good working capital management also signals a strong financial discipline to your various stakeholders, which will be invaluable in any current or future capital-raising effort.

Exercise the strictest financial discipline.

T he type of business model you choose has a direct effect on how you should finance your venture. Clearly your monthly burn rate should always be minimized, but certain plans will require very different organizational priorities than others. An edict often issued by panicked venture capitalists during downturns in the business cycle—that you must immediately reduce your burn rate to a set limit or face imminent death—is, frankly, foolish. Yes, in bad times, reduce your burn rate, but by how much is largely determined by what business you are in and what stage in its development your business is at.

A mobile application company, for instance, will generally burn much less cash than a life science company searching for a cure for cancer or a rocket company taking aim at Mars. The risk-return profile changes, so this is not a matter of the monthly cash burn in the absolute sense, but rather an indication of whether the plan is reasonable and financeable in the eye of a potential investor.

Some businesses simply may not be able to manage a significant retrenchment of expenditures, because they have large fixed costs and will have to cease all operations below a certain spending threshold. Understand up front whether you are entering into an Evel Knievel business model (after the 1970s motorcycle daredevil known for jumping across rows of trucks, pits of rattlesnakes, and vast canyons), one that requires large influxes of capital to get airborne, without any place to land until you touch down at threshold scale on the other side, and manage your financing strategy accordingly. A business like this simply may not be able to survive a major market downturn unless it has already reached positive unit economics, so you will need to raise as much capital as you can, whenever you can, and stash it away like a squirrel fearing a cold winter.

A good example of the different business cultures that various business models instill is the contrast between the financial discipline practiced by an old-school semiconductor-manufacturing company and that employed by an online consumer software developer. The semiconductor firms have high fixed costs, low margins, and little free capital, and as such they require the strictest financial discipline. They watch and take care of every penny. A small mistake can be fatal, and pivots are not likely, given their burn rates. At the other end of the spectrum is the online consumer software developer, with huge gross margins, in an industry where the outcome is often almost binary (the product either gets adopted or not), and as such, their financial discipline is a lower priority as they pursue a boom-or-bust mentality.

It is important to remember that the financial culture of a venture will be directly driven by (a) its financial and business planning processes, (b) its leadership, and (c) its financial discipline. In startups, the financial culture is often ignored as so many investors pile cash into low-capital businesses like software and online services, hoping to drive the business to dominance and defensible scale quickly. Damn the cash flow and profits—they will come after you have achieved scale. The laws of capital supply and demand inflate the valuations of these ventures, thereby reducing the return on investment in spite of the lower capital requirement. So it can benefit contrarian investors to adopt a stricter financial discipline and look for more difficult but potentially more rewarding challenges.

RULE 23

Always be frugal.

I t is so important to hire people who are frugal by nature. As they say, you are what you do when nobody is watching. If you hire frugal people, your culture will benefit. You won't have to control or fight costs continuously, rely on process rather than ethos, or turn your finance team into bad cops, thus eroding the company's culture. In larger companies, many processes are instituted precisely to assure that people are doing the right thing. But those processes bring overhead in terms of management, costs, and delays, and they are anathema to the empowerment and creativity required to innovate. It's a fine balance between discipline and creativity. So when you are small, rely more on culture than on processes and policing. Everyone will rue the day the balance shifts from culture to process; that's the day your most entrepreneurial talent will move on to more creative pastures.

Unfortunately, the reality for many startups is that as soon as you have over, say, thirty people in the company, costs seem to increase disproportionally. Typically, between two-thirds and three-quarters of all operating expenses are headcount related expenses. Therefore, to control costs you should start by focusing on your staffing levels. Hire frugally and stay lean.

As CEO you should approve all requisitions before they are

opened. This creates a hurdle for anyone wanting to hire. If they can't justify it to you they won't try. Save on roles wherever you can and only invest in new positions where it is prudent and necessary. Such frugality should be demonstrated from the very top; you must set the example at all times. If your people observe you signing off on new headcount and expenses willy-nilly they will do the same. Every contract with an attorney, a printer, an accountant, a consultant, and so on should be reviewed, sharpened, and challenged, and each party should be held accountable for the work. Set the example and the rest of the company will follow.

A Japanese executive at a large company made a practice of sending back every expense report to his subordinates with a question about some minor inconsistency, a seemingly immaterial decimal point. While the subordinates wondered why their boss would waste time on trivial matters, they nevertheless scrutinized their own accounts thoroughly and became more precise and accurate. The executive revealed later that his actions were purely intended to set a cultural standard. He actually did not review every item of their accounts; he would instead skim them to identify a discrepancy or two. Then he would send their reports back with a question about them. He knew that if they perceived him as having the time to spend scrutinizing the smallest costs, so would his team. Counting your pennies and running "lean" is not determined by how much you spend, but by how you spend it. It will cost a lot more to build a precious metal refinery than a gossip website, but that doesn't mean each venture should not be frugal in everything it does.

To get where you are going, you need to know where you are going.

The early days of a startup are electric with energy and devoid of process. You use sheer force of will to figure things out. It may not look pretty, but you are making progress. You need to be very clear on which aspects of the business you are hacking for the sake of expediency but expect to fix later, and which aspects you are building to last. For instance, investing in receivables collection or customer support automation may not make sense until you have a demonstrable business, but investing in sturdy and scalable platform technology may be necessary from the start in order to accelerate the speed of development in the long run.

Consequently, as your business matures, one of your many responsibilities is to determine the right measurement structure for clarifying the venture's (1) objectives, (2) schedule, (3) progress, and (4) accountability. You should aim to target and remove different risks depending on the stage of the product and the commercial cycle. By measuring, you focus the team like a laser on those critical goals; by not measuring, you signal that other goals are not as important.

In order to successfully execute a staged financing strategy—one where you raise enough money to remove the current white-hot risks and then go back to the market to raise more, at a higher valuation, in order to address the next-level risks—the precision of these measuring tools is absolutely crucial. Your financing strategy depends on it, because if you are measuring the wrong things, you will waste critical time and resources without removing risk and increasing your value. The better the execution, according to its predicted measures and plan, the exponentially greater the chances of success for the venture in both performance and fundraising.

It goes without saying that the plan should be the team's plan, not just the CEO's plan. There needs to be complete buy-in if empowerment and accountability are to work. The type of business and the stage of the venture are the primary factors in deciding what to measure, how much to measure, and in what way to measure.

Remember that success starts from doing one thing very well—then broadening as appropriate. The purpose of any form of performance metrics is to identify where the venture needs to go in a specific time frame and then determine how you will measure to see whether the venture is getting there. What will those interim steps look like, and how will you define success along the way?

You start by identifying your core business assumptions. These are what you need to measure. Now decide what the appropriate metrics should be in any future period if you are going to be on track. These are your targets. For example, if your business is dependent on attracting customers with a lifetime value three times greater than your costs of marketing to them, you should measure customer lifetime value (LTV) and customer acquisition costs (CAC) carefully to keep on plan. If they deviate from expectation, you need to react. Without measuring, there is no way to know your progress, and without knowing your progress, how can you learn, improve, and adapt? The faster this doing, measuring, learning, and refining cycle is, the more competitive you will be.

To support such an exercise, it helps to develop a defined set of business practices that are nonnegotiable and to set clear limits. Otherwise, smart people will game the system and your measurements will be skewed. For example, are you willing to do exclusive deals with your customers, or do you prefer to stay open to all opportunities? If you are measuring revenues per customer, your salespeople may choose to close a few lucrative exclusive deals. If you are measuring the number of new customers, your salespeople may choose to enter into relatively cheap but quick nonexclusive deals. Be clear and firm, or you may end up with exactly the wrong result. Knowing what you are *not* doing is every bit as important as knowing your collective goals.

For more information about how to implement objectives and key results, we recommend John Doerr's *Measure What Matters*.

Measurement comes with pitfalls.

The challenge in applying prematurely strict measurement principles is the danger of locking the company into assumptions that might not prove true. Key performance indicators (KPIs) and objectives and key results (OKRs) that are too rigid can effectively become a straitjacket for your venture. At the early stages, you should focus on flexible dashboards for methodically guiding experimentation to test assumptions before committing fully to achieving them. This means experimenting not only with your technology or product assumptions, but also with assumptions about your market, customers, value proposition, channels of distribution, and so on. It is as important to disprove wrong assumptions as it is to establish a measurable operating plan.

If your initial five-year business plan—a plan created before you have profits or revenues or customers, and often before you have a product or service—turns out to be accurate, you are lucky, not smart. You don't yet have enough information to be smart. And while it is often said that it is better to be lucky than smart, you and your investors can't count on luck. So you want to become smarter as quickly as you can. And that means making informed assumptions and testing them quickly and cheaply. Rely on intuition—not just seat-of-your-pants intuition, but rather the informed-by-data intuition—and keep measuring constantly to be sure.

Start by articulating your assumptions, particularly your "leap of faith" assumptions, which are essential to the success of your business. What are your leaps of faith? To answer that question, you start by critically evaluating your idea and your plan and identifying the things that must be true for them to work. Then you research related ideas and businesses, past and present, to understand what made them succeed or fail. Don't believe that you are the only one to travel down this road. Others have surely tried related things, or aspects of them.

The cheapest, quickest progress you can make is to learn from the successes and failures of others. For instance, Apple probably learned a lot about portable personal music players from the success of the Sony Walkman and the failure of Napster. The ventures that succeed become your analogs, the case studies that prove some critical assumption in your plan. The ones that fail become your antilogs, the case studies that show flaws in your assumptions and that lead you to gather more information or refine your plan. Finally, there will be critical, life-or-death assumptions that you cannot answer through research alone and which you will need to test directly through trial and error. These are your leaps of faith.

Now design simple, quick, cheap, measurable "tests" to validate or disprove your leaps of faith. Remember: determining that an assumption is wrong is as much of a "success" as validating an assumption, so long as you respond quickly and refine accordingly. Do it now, while mistakes are cheap, rather than find yourself having spent valuable time and money proceeding down a dead end. After you resolve your immediate leaps of faith, you will uncover new ones as your business evolves. Keep running a focused dashboarding process to identify, test, measure, and refine.

Only when your venture has demonstrable proof of its product and its market should it consider more rigid metrics like balanced scorecards and OKRs. If you lock down your plan and metrics too early, you risk committing yourself to an unsuccessful path or, just as costly, a suboptimal path that delivers some, but insufficient, success. The latter is the most dangerous, because the early results may lull you into believing your assumptions are correct when in fact they aren't.

Operational setbacks require swift and deep cutbacks.

The best advice when encountering the inevitable operational setbacks is to be decisive, and to cut early and deep so you can live to fight another day. Make a quick pivot or pause and run new dashboard tests to find your next path, but do it decisively. Entrepreneurs who have experienced their fair share of operational setbacks frequently mention that one of their biggest regrets is that they cut too late or not deep enough when they had the chance. If, after weathering a cutback, you are forced to cut again, your stakeholders will lose confidence and your employees will desert you. There are few truisms in business, but this is one to remember: whenever you choose to cut or change course, you will always wish you had done so earlier. After all, the information was there all the time. Why did you ignore it? Was it stubbornness or wishful thinking? You can't get that precious time or money back.

Inexperienced operators may feel that by cutting deep, they are leaving value on the cutting-room floor, but if you don't move decisively, you will be leaving _all_ your value on the floor. You need to think like an emergency first responder arriving at a crash site. Calmly review the situation, prioritize, and then attend to each of the "patients" or opportunities, focusing relentlessly on your core competencies. Stop the bleeding (of cash), and buy time to get on the right path, even if it means you must cease debt service, renegotiate accounts payables, and so on. If you have the cash in hand, you are in control for the moment. Use it judiciously.

A good example is a public company that ran into an ugly cash crunch. The company was making large debt payments to a big strategic investor that was represented on the board by its CEO. One of the seasoned old hands on the board reviewed the company financials projected on the boardroom screen, pointed to the debt service line, and said to the CEO of the strategic investor, sitting next to him, "Obviously we are not going to make those payments until we are out of the woods. So what can we do for you in exchange for a moratorium?" The CEO was shocked and indignant, knowing that he would have to explain this to his own board, but he ultimately conceded.

Possession is sometimes nine-tenths of the law, with the remainder being a tangle of lawyers and litigation fees. Your cash—that is, the cash you have in hand—is oxygen for your venture, and in a dire situation you need to act fast to preserve every breath. If you survive this crisis, you can make it up to your creditors later. Now is not the time to be nice; it is the time to be effective and resolute in order to survive.

Save surprises for birthdays, not for your stakeholders.

D ue to their strongly optimistic nature, early-stage investors in particular are often caught off guard when a venture starts missing its plan, initiates a downward spiral, or needs to pivot. Even when the signs have been apparent for some time before the actual crisis begins, it is not an uncommon reaction. Your job is to deliver the bad news to your investors—but how?

Because you are wrestling with the issues and reviewing the metrics every day, and you are intimately aware of the challenges as they unfold, you may believe that your board should know them as well. But the fact is that most board members spend only a few hours a month thinking about your business, so the situation might not be as obvious to them. Moreover, many early-stage investors lack sufficient entrepreneurial experience and think they invested in a fixed plan rather than in a team running a grand experiment. They may be shocked when the plan does not come to fruition. There's always a risk that what you believe you are saying and what investors are hearing or want to hear are out of whack. Running through the dashboard process (the game plan for testing assumptions, complete with specific metrics and responses) with your entire board, so that they understand what you are testing, what you are learning, and when you are refining, helps avoid potential misunderstandings.

Don't wait for board meetings to share critical information. Consider providing a key performance indicator (KPI) report weekly or monthly, with historical and plan comparisons and commentary to keep everyone on the same page.

In times of crisis, misalignments can lead to delays in critical decisions as your directors, investors, and lenders come up to speed and perform their own independent reviews of your situation. Continuous, frank communication helps maintain alignment and supports fast action when time is of the essence. Make sure to never surprise your directors in a board meeting. You need to keep your constituencies informed by email, in person, and via phone calls along the way. Especially when there is a crisis, you should conduct one-on-one informational meetings with each of your directors so you can tailor the message and address their particular concerns in advance of critical board decisions. Yes, this is time-consuming, but maintaining trusting relationships with your stakeholders is essential at every stage, especially since there's little doubt that in the future you'll hit new roadblocks and new turning points that will require board and investor support.

RULE 28

Strategic pivots offer silver linings.

In a crisis, savvy investors are looking for a rational, capital-efficient plan they can support. The question you need to be able to answer for your investors is whether you can emerge from crisis with an attractive, sustainable business and a leadership team fully committed to making it happen. It's your job to prepare such a plan and demonstrate that commitment, not to simply beg their indulgence while you pray for the storm clouds to pass. As Warren Buffett says, "When a management [or an investor] with a reputation for brilliance tackles a business with a reputation for bad economics, it is the reputation of the business that remains intact." Is the failing business the result of one-time circumstances and bad luck? Or the result of a poor business model and an unachievable plan? These are two very different situations and require very different approaches from you.

If your business is still compelling but needs to execute a significant strategic pivot, it may well require retreating to recapitalize the business at a substantially lower valuation. Maintaining a higher valuation through a bridge loan or an insider round (where your existing investors cough up more money, but no new investor comes to the table to validate the price) might simply not make sense and can complicate your ultimate realignment by setting the wrong incentives and capitalization framework. A pivot point can be, paradoxically, a great opportunity: fatigued investors can step back and sell their shares, while new investors can be secured to finance the venture's new strategy. Don't view pivots as a defeat; it's just another puzzle you need to solve so you can create new value for the company and the remaining stakeholders.

Solve for success, not dilution. If board members are seeking to step down or investors are looking to step away from the venture when things become difficult, then it is best to let them go. A good new investor will understand that fund dynamics can drive tired investors out, and that someone else's selling opportunity is their buying opportunity.

While pivots are par for the course, don't get into the habit of making diving catches to resuscitate your business. Companies that appear to pivot too frequently make investors and their employees dizzy and erode stakeholder support over time.

PART 2

SELECTING THE RIGHT INVESTORS

P art 1 set out a game plan for establishing the fundamentals for a successful and lasting business.

The rules in part 2 are about choosing the best investors for your venture. Fit is critical. Everyone seems to covet venture capital, but is it really right for you? And if it is, how do you select the right investor? Incubators are all the rage, but would you benefit from participating? And strategic investors may offer a strong shoulder in the storm, but they bring a host of tricky considerations. Whatever you do, do your homework. Choose a partner whom you connect with at both a personal level and a values level. Be sure their reputation is warranted. Each investor has their own particular goals and attributes, so the quality of the fit is paramount to your success.

RULE 29

Don't accept money from strangers.

Your mother was right: be suspicious of strangers bearing gifts. When the capital markets are overheated, you are likely to meet a diverse array of investors seeking to ride your shirttails to the big payoff. Never mind that the payoff is almost as elusive as real unicorns—portfolio investors can afford to fail a lot in order to be part of some random huge success. The sad fact is that the clear majority of venture funds will not even return the capital they have raised from their limited partners during their ten-year lives. In spite of all the headlines, it's interesting to contemplate who actually makes money in the startup business. Most entrepreneurs fail, most venture capitalists fail, but the economics of winning are so powerful that for a lucky few, it overwhelms the averages. Desperate gamblers whose portfolios are falling behind can't resist investing in a highflier with a huge nominal valuation, even if there is no business in sight. In poker, when the "pot odds"—the size of the pot versus the size of bet needed to stay in the hand—mesmerizes the gamblers to the point that they forget the actual probabilities of winning, it is reason for concern.

You need to do everything you can to increase your odds of being one of the lucky winners. Start by choosing your partners carefully. And that's what your early investors are: your partners. They bring much more than cash; they bring experience and connections. If they have the skills and judgment, they can make a big difference. You need to plant your seed in rich soil and do everything you can to optimize the conditions for success. Your investors and board members are crucial ingredients. Carefully select the best stakeholders you can and set up the conditions to motivate them to go the extra mile for you.

Don't just take the first eager investor who knocks at your door. Explore your options fully. The best entrepreneurs are always making the time and effort to meet potential stakeholders well in advance of needing money. They are raising money every day, even if they haven't asked for the check yet. In this way, they can vet the field for the best match. Great fundraisers are proactive, not reactive, and they don't take money from strangers.

RULE 30

Incubators are good for finding investors, not for developing businesses.

Incubators have been around for decades and can be found all across the planet. They are places where entrepreneurs can work side by side and receive advice and tap into networks to develop their ideas into fundable ventures.

Y Combinator is perhaps the most famous incubator, because of the companies it has spawned—Airbnb, Dropbox, Zenefits, and Stripe among them. Y Combinator runs two programs a year in the San Francisco Bay Area, each three months long, where entrepreneurs share space as they develop their ideas. It ends in a Demo Day where the graduates present their business plans to a host of venture capitalists. Their hit rate for financings is very high.

Some incubators specialize in particular fields, like health care or renewable energy; others are more ecumenical. The consensus among investors is that, while they do little to help you create great businesses, they do grant degrees in killer pitches. And their alumni, like those of any good business school, are active and supportive of one another. Moreover, they will get you an audience with investors.

The story goes that one Y Combinator venture changed to an entirely different business the week of Demo Day, simply repurposing the graphs and charts from its previous pitch, even though the businesses were wholly unrelated. Still, the charts showed perfect hockey sticks without labels on either axis, soaring up and to the right to indicate their ultimate huge market acceptance, the hallmark of a Y Combinator pitch. And even with the unrelated charts, they were still able to raise money from investors on the day of their presentation. Whether it's true or not, you get the point—an incubator can be a good substitute for a network when looking for investors.

Avoid venture capital unless you absolutely need it.

With all the media hype around venture capital, startups, and so-called unicorns, one would think that venture capital was always the best way to fund your venture. After all, unlike other sources of capital, like debt and friends and family, venture capitalists appreciate the vagaries and risks inherent in starting a business and offer more than money to assist in your success. Venture capitalists are sometimes lionized for their extraordinary financial outcomes, as if they created that success themselves, which would be like the suits in the skyboxes celebrating with the players in the end zone after a touchdown (for you American football neophytes, that's when the players thump their chests and do silly antics on the field after scoring). But be skeptical.

Remember: venture capital comes at a price, in the form of a meaningful percentage of your company. Perversely, the less you sell them, the less skin they have in the game and the less time and "value-added" attention you are likely to receive in return. So you have to be prepared to part with a significant portion of your company to even attract a good venture capitalist. You aren't just raising money; you are selling ownership.

With that ownership come a host of governance terms and

concessions. Venture capitalists will impose certain controls on what you can and cannot do without their approval, such as sell the company or issue new shares. You will be asked to vest ownership of your own shares over time to align your incentives with theirs, even if you already own them all outright.

And most often, the lead venture capitalist will demand board representation. Moreover, they will usually create a board that leaves you with a minority vote. As board members, they will have a broad array of powers over your day-to-day business, including even the power to fire you and hire your replacement. You aren't just adding a partner; you are hiring your boss.

Venture capital rewards its limited-partner investors—those endowments, pension funds, and wealthy individuals who give them money to invest—with distributions of stock and cash from their successful investments. Without those distributions, venture capitalists cannot raise their next fund, which they will, in turn, invest in even more startups. When you accept venture capital, you are accepting the responsibility to deliver your investors liquidity in publicly tradable stock or cash within a reasonable period, likely four to six years. If you are not interested in pursuing liquidity, or don't yet know, then you are not a good candidate for venture capital.

And venture capital brings a penchant for scaling businesses. This may be the very reason you are seeking venture capital, but consider it carefully. You have all your eggs in one basket. Venture capitalists have a portfolio of eggs. More and more, the venture capital industry is chasing unicorns and black swans to pay for their broken eggs. True, venture capitalists may be more willing to roll the dice on your business, for the chance of creating an extraordinary outcome to juice their portfolio returns. This may be good in theory, but if you have a longer-term view than theirs, there will be plenty of room for disagreements down the road about how much risk to take and how quickly to scale.

Finally, ask yourself whether your business is at a stage where you can really put venture capital to good use. If you are able to sort out your leap-of-faith risks (your life-or-death assumptions about your business) without an institutional investment, then it may be preferable to do that before considering venture capital—in other words, you can self-fund your growth. If you haven't taken venture capital and your early efforts prove fruitless, you can walk away easily. If, instead, you find traction, you will be better able to attract top-shelf venture capital on favorable terms.

For all their promises of bringing more than money, many venture capitalists don't deliver on their "value-added services." Don't take all their marketing messages at face value. But the best venture capitalists can provide you with an unfair advantage in recruiting people, making strategic connections, raising more capital and debt, elevating your visibility, and establishing your credibility. Be certain they will deliver what you need most when you need it.

And venture capitalists can be fickle. Because they manage a portfolio of investments, it behooves them to spend their time, money, and attention on the ventures that offer the best chances of returns, not those struggling to find direction. They will love you when they write the check, but will they be there when things get tough? If they aren't, it can send a negative signal to employees, potential investors, and other stakeholders.

You may have access to other, more manageable sources of capital, like customers who will pay you as you go or in advance. If you can achieve positive cash flows quickly without deviating from your core strategy and slowing down development, then it may not make sense to raise money from venture capitalists, with all the commensurate headaches. Perhaps you can find a shell of a company with a bad idea and money in the bank that you can merge with your good idea and take in a new direction. Maybe you are able to run a crowdfunding campaign to raise enough money to prove your concept. There are lots of ways to find a little capital.

To be sure, most entrepreneurs never raise venture capital. On the other hand, most highly valued, successful ventures do. And even those ventures that grow for years without venture capital often bring it in later when their interests in scale and liquidity align well with venture capital.

Venture capital can bring experience, connections, mentoring, and the invaluable skills for developing an idea into a business and an entrepreneur into a successful leader. It may be an imperfect choice but nevertheless the best one for your business. So choose wisely and know what you are getting.

RULE 32

If you choose venture capital, pick the right type of investor.

There are roughly nine hundred venture firms in the United States alone, and probably three or four times that number of venture capitalists. Add to that the people in hedge funds, offshore funds, and corporate funds, and other investors looking for early-stage companies, and you can appreciate the challenge in categorizing the types of venture capitalists. So at the risk of offending someone, we submit that venture capitalists generally fit into one of the following broad categories.

THEMATIC INVESTORS: These venture capitalists study trends and scour the field to arrive at their own theses about where the big opportunities lie. They analyze, pontificate, and put their money where their mouths are. They tend to proactively pursue ventures that are consistent with these theses, and they focus their time and energies accordingly. They are easy to identify, because they talk openly and often about where they see the next big thing. If you fit their thesis, you are likely a good candidate for an investment. If you don't, you aren't. The good news is that thematic investors can bring outspoken strategic input and market intelligence to your venture. The downside is that they may prefer their own judgment on such things over yours.

DOMAIN INVESTORS: These venture capitalists usually have business experience in a particular industry, such as semiconductors, health care, or financial services ("fintech"). They look for ventures addressing those industries because it's what they know, essentially looking for their keys under the lights. The good news is that if your venture is in an industry that a domain investor is pursuing, it is a natural fit. They can bring a wealth of industry experience and connections to your venture. The downside is that they may be prisoners of their own experience and resistant to your new, industry-disrupting ideas.

QUANT INVESTORS: These venture capitalists, like their hedge fund namesakes, rely on hard data to guide them. This is a more recent phenomenon, coincident with the rise of big data, social media, and online tracking. As a result, they tend to be younger. They collect and analyze reams of up-to-the-minute metrics to identify emerging ventures, sort of like the *Billboard* music charts that showed trending songs and musicians in the analog days—but now with computers and algorithms. These venture capitalists are aggressive and don't need to know much more about you and your business than the numbers. They jump on trending metrics and look for inflection points that give them conviction before your financial results are predictable enough for growth investors. The good news is that quant investors are diligent students of growth and can bring that perspective and those skills to your business, helping you to use all the available digital growth tools to full advantage. The bad news is that they often have no operating instincts and provide little help with strategy or execution.

PEOPLE INVESTORS: These venture capitalists are rather old-school. So old that they are new again. They don't presuppose that they are smarter than the herd of entrepreneurs exploring new horizons, so they don't rely on their own theses. They may have had expertise in a specific domain, but their venture experience has transcended that and they have been forced to stray into unknown territory. They like numbers, but they realize that at the earliest stages, the numbers are unreliable and often lie. So they resort to what time and experience have given them: the ability to judge the quality and character of people. They get their ideas from listening to a never-ending stream of entrepreneurs explaining their vision for solving particular problems. If your problem is interesting and big enough, and your solution is novel and likely to be highly valued by customers, and you have the intelligence, grit, moxie, and passion to be a great leader, then you may be a good fit for this investor. The good news is that people investors value talent highly and are anxious to invest themselves in you and your team. They see the challenge through a human lens; it's not enough for the company to be successful— they hope to get the founders, the investors, and the company across the finish line together. The bad news is that they may not be particularly expert at any one thing that you need.

GROWTH INVESTORS: These investors specialize in later-stage ventures, though they may dabble in startups as well. They are strong financial analysts and run detailed models to test business plan sensitivities. Because of that, they generally want you to have substantial financial data before they invest, and they want to see enough operating history to convince them that the data is meaningful. As a rule of thumb, you need to be doing at least $10 million of annual revenue before you can get the attention of a U.S. growth investor. After careful analysis, they bet on changes in the trajectory of your growth curves over time. The good news is that growth investors are adept financial architects and can be very helpful in preparing your company for eventual liquidity. The bad news is that they tend to be analysts, not operators, and their input is skewed accordingly.

All five types of venture capitalists can be successful investors. And depending on fit and chemistry, all five can be constructive board members and partners. Just know what type of venture capitalist you want, so you know how to extract the most value from them.

RULE 33

Conduct detailed due diligence on your investors.

You are about to get into a long-term partnership with an investor, so you'd better make sure to conduct a detailed background check. We will avoid the cliché relationship analogies here and just say do your homework. Whenever possible, meet their portfolio company CEOs and even CFOs, and any ex-associates and former partners, to get honest references. What is their fund size? How much has already been invested? How much dry powder will they keep for your venture, and do they support follow-on rounds? Do they ever lead in follow-on rounds? What is their definition of success (2× returns? 10× returns? somewhere in between?), and how have they dealt with disappointments in the past: Do they support founders or jettison them when the going gets tough?

And make sure you talk to their failed ventures, not just their winners. Ask for specific examples of how they have helped ventures and founders who are at a similar stage or in a similar industry, and, more important, find out how they have dealt with setbacks or changes to the plan. Dumb money is plentiful, and the terms and ease of closing may seem attractive, but smart money will add value, work with you to overcome challenges, and roll up its sleeves when needed. Smart money should be accretive to you even at lower valuations.

Remember that it is the partner at the firm who will be most important to you, not the partnership itself. The investment firm is of secondary value, provided your lead partner has the clout to tap the firm's resources. The right partner understands that business plans are dynamic and embraces course corrections that address new information and opportunities. The right partner is more important than the valuation. After all, you wouldn't hire a mediocre executive for your team just because he or she is cheaper than the alternative. You want the best person you can hire for every position in your venture. Someone who can be a game changer, not just a cheerleader. When choosing an investor, do not settle for less.

RULE 34

Personal wealth ≠ good investing.

Consider a famous venture capitalist who was quizzed by an aspiring entrepreneur about how successful he's been: "I know this game and I can help you. Look at my track record. It was the late nineties; we were inexperienced and simply scratched out our business plan on a napkin. Venture capitalists fought to invest. We didn't even ship a product before we went public during the 1999 tech bubble. Our stock tripled the first day, and within six months AOL gobbled us up for a big premium. All of a sudden, I'm twenty-two years young and worth $60 million. Now, after a couple decades of venture investing, I'm worth over $80 million. I have the Midas touch."

Okay. Well, let's do the math: sure, he hit the jackpot in 1999, but since then his investments have generated a gain of only $20 million in about seventeen years. Which is roughly a 1.7 percent annual return, while inflation averaged over 2 percent. Even Treasury bills, one of the most trusted and therefore conservative securities, have yielded between 1.6 percent and more than 6 percent per year during that same period. So his claim to success is a company that never shipped a product or made a dollar, an IPO in an irrationally exuberant market, a fortuitous sale of the company just before the tech bubble crashed, and subsequent investment returns that trail the lowly Treasury bill yields.

And even respected investors who were, in fact, brilliant at moments in the market cycle can lose their touch. A bull in a bull market is a beautiful thing, but a bull in a bear market is not pretty. Wealth and fame are not necessarily correlated with intelligence—or with investing acumen. We are programmed to look for cause whenever there is an effect, but sometimes there just isn't one. Luck is hard to replicate.

Instead, choose an investor who can bring you experience and support your venture's needs. Find someone who has been through business cycles and is still standing. Look for someone who has been able to apply their experience across industries and technologies as things change, which they always do. Favor good judgment over personal scorecards, because you will never know how much the scorecard reflects acumen and intelligence versus just plain luck.

————————

Choose investors who think like operators.

Successful venture capital investors should have three characteristics: (1) a strong network that provides good deal flow, (2) sound judgment, and (3) the ability to develop an investment and its founder to a successful outcome. Let's see how those skills align with your needs.

Deal flow and network refer to the investor's access to interesting founders, ideas, talent, and partners through their community of investments, advisers, co-investors, experts, strategic partners, and so on. Can the investor's network be helpful to your ability to recruit the best talent, for example? Do they have connections among strategic partners who can invest, help co-develop, or even buy your venture at some point? Can the investor's credibility help you attract customers and funding in subsequent rounds?

Sound judgment relates to their ability to choose the best ventures to invest in, not to guiding you in making the best decisions for your business. Their nose for investments tells you nothing about whether they can help you day-to-day, a factor to consider carefully if they are demanding a board seat with their investment.

Given strong networks and good judgment, there still

remains another, even more important aspect of the investor's qualifying characteristics: Does the investor have the operating experience and skills to develop you and your business to a successful outcome? Do they have the character to support you and your team in good times and bad? And is there the right chemistry between you and the investor to create a relationship of trust, respect, and confidence?

Too often, venture investing is characterized as a sort of lottery in which a few spectacular wins make up for the unfortunate body count of failures. More and more investors pursue a portfolio strategy based on sheer statistics, rather than the ability to build any single compelling business.

And indeed, too often investors are unable to work with the management of a fledgling venture when the inevitable operating problems occur, because they simply don't have the prerequisite experience. Ever since the "invention" of the venture model, pretty much every portfolio company at every venture investment firm has at one time or another faced troubles requiring close and active involvement from its board and investors. Consequently, the investing partner's operating experience is an important qualification. It's a good policy to never take money from a lead investor who has not had to make payroll themselves. Otherwise they won't fully appreciate what you are going through.

For their partners in the firm, VCs need to think like investors first and operators second. But for you, they must be an operator first and an investor second. You are not choosing a great investor; you are choosing a skilled business partner.

The best investor in the world may not be able to help you succeed unless they bring more to the table than their track record. Ensure that your investors have survived good times and bad and have the backbone and stamina to help you make the hard decisions when you face them.

RULE 36

Deal directly with the decision makers.

Venture capital firms vary in size, but by and large they are collections of investing professionals and associates. The associates may have fancy titles, but they don't have the authority to make investment decisions. Focus on engaging with the decision makers, not the foot soldiers. Too many entrepreneurs waste their time with junior people at investment firms. Entrepreneurs may be flattered that a top-notch firm has cold-called them to learn about their business, but the sad truth is that, most often, the person who called is just gathering information on you and all of your competitors. Junior people are often deputized to troll for opportunities without a license to hunt. It's only a scintilla of interest, so refuse to spend significant time in due diligence unless the decision makers are present and engaged. Your time is more precious than theirs.

The junior people can be quite smart, and they may be excellent at spotting market trends and tracking breakout opportunities, but they probably lack experience from which to critically judge your venture's potential. As a result, a false start with an associate may unnecessarily color the firm's first impression of your venture. If you are going to make a first impression, make it with a decision maker. After any preliminary discussion with the junior folks, ask for a meeting with the decision makers if the talks are to continue.

If you are already in the firm's portfolio and you find the firm substituting an associate for an investing partner on your board, be wary. You are at risk of becoming an "orphaned investment." No matter how eager the replacement is, they are likely to have insufficient stature within their partnership to get you the attention and resources you need. This is especially critical for subsequent financing decisions. In those moments, it is important to regain the good grace and attention of the decision makers of the fund to ensure continued support.

Find stable investors.

We both have seen how investors can, in very short order, make big shifts in their strategy, such as shifts from investing heavily in, for example, life science or consumer hardware to investing in mobile apps or enterprise software. It's not an accident that investors have been unfavorably compared to lemmings. And personnel shifts may occur within partnerships if some partners leave the firm for greener pastures mid–funding cycle.

The same applies to growth investors who may momentarily quench their venture capital envy by sticking their toe in early-stage ventures, only to exit just as quickly when the water turns frigid, and to strategic investors who change their investment strategy every time their company modifies its business strategy. Often, these investors think they can outperform proven venture capitalists. And when they are unable to pick, win, or build, they will rapidly withdraw from sight. It is a lot easier to invest in later-stage businesses where you have strong performance metrics to guide you than it is to pick early-stage entrepreneurs and opportunities where there is no track record to draw from.

As ventures inevitably get into operational trouble over

time or face longer gestation periods as private companies, the patience and stability of the investors, as well as access to follow-on capital, is paramount. Partner with people and organizations you can rely on for the long term, or at least as long as you need to become successful.

RULE 38

Select investors who can help future financings.

A conscious and well-executed first fundraise will lay the groundwork for significantly easier subsequent raises. Be mindful that with each fundraise, you are not just raising precious capital, but you are also adding evangelists and potential sources of additional capital. The warm introductions that insiders can provide will go a very long way in establishing your credibility and in bringing good investors into subsequent rounds. Investors with similar interests tend to know one another, and they gravitate toward friendly syndicates, essentially sharing in the sourcing and funding of their common interests. If you can, bring the right partner from one of the leading investment firms onto your board in an earlier round so that they can bring their network of investors to later capital raises.

Having said that, you may think it would be ideal to have an early lead investor who will fund all of your future requirements, alleviating the need to spend precious time on lengthy fundraises—in effect, one-stop shopping. But while this may allow you to focus on your business rather than fundraising, it also creates something of an investor monoculture. You end up with only one source of advice and direction, a single point of view on you and your business. And as good as this investor may be, multiple heads are better than one. Furthermore, if things go sour, you are completely dependent on one firm and its sentiment rather than a diversity of perspectives. This could create a dangerously narrow funding base, causing a financing risk if your single source of capital cannot or will not support you when you need it. And with only one investor, there is no market pressure on later-round pricing and terms.

Mind you, no one was complaining at WhatsApp when Facebook bought it for nearly $20 billion after Sequoia Capital led every round. Nevertheless, you may be trading too much value for convenience. Building effective syndicates usually pays dividends later.

RULE 39

Investor syndicates need to be managed.

Within investor syndicates, co-investors frequently expect the lead investor to carry the water for the venture and consequently don't invest enough soft capital in your success. They don't spend the time between meetings or marshal their firm's resources and connections.

This is particularly troublesome when no single investor has sufficient ownership to act as the lead. When investors insist on purchasing a particular ownership percentage of your venture, you should insist that they invest their time and leadership in return. Without a strong lead, you are likely to spend a lot of time managing internal investor politics and herding venture capitalists.

Don't confuse your lead investor and your lead director. Your lead investor is the one who sets the terms of a funding round and also often takes a board seat. The lead director, who may or may not be your lead investor as well, is the one charged with coordinating the board and liaising with you.

Syndicates often act like committees or large convoys, with the slowest member determining your overall speed. Having a larger syndicate of investors is not necessarily a bad thing, but you should select the group carefully, provide sufficient ownership for a motivated lead, and spend adequate time with each investor to assure they add the value you expect. This can be solved to some extent by articulating your expectations of each investor and working closely with the lead investor to achieve those expectations.

The lead investor should, in turn, commit sufficient time and energy to leading the shareholders and be held accountable for their overall contribution. You need to form a close bond with the lead investor, because they are your envoy to the syndicate, and the syndicate's envoy to you.

RULE 40

Capital-intensive ventures require deep financial pockets.

Complex and capital-intensive ventures are even more likely than most to hit setbacks, incur delays, and require more money than originally anticipated. For example, value creation in biotech is costly. Most of the value is created after the issuance of regulatory approvals following a long, uncertain, and expensive set of trials. Consequently, in biotech, a lot of the pretrial funding comes from either large syndicates of specialized investors or big pharmaceutical companies that strategically invest, for access to innovation, while providing both the money and the expertise for navigating the regulatory process. You can't control the clock, so you need your investors to help fund possible delays and setbacks. An important qualifier for this group of investors, therefore, will be their susceptibility to "deal fatigue," a malady whereby investors are not resilient but rather expect execution in accordance with the plan and within a disproportionately short time frame. Firms specializing in seed-stage investing or consumer software are a poor fit for biotech.

Hardware ventures similarly require deep pockets. They take longer to develop proof-of-concept products, cost more to operate, and require significant working capital for inventories, etc. They have less opportunity to pivot, because of their commensurately high burn rates. In this day and age of digital everything, there are still a few investors who have the discipline to invest in great hardware innovation and offer the deep pockets to see it through. Always make sure your investors are appropriate for your industry, venture risk, commercialization time frame, and reward profile. An unhappy investor only makes your already difficult job harder.

RULE 41

Strategic investors pose unique challenges.

Corporations flush with cash and short on innovation are frequent investors in startups. They offer know-how, resources, validation, and potential mergers-and-acquisitions exits in addition to their investments. Sometimes they also partner with startups to provide specific business opportunities inside their own businesses and can serve as your beachhead customer.

This can sound pretty attractive, and occasionally it is. But taking money from a strategic investor is tricky.

First, the stage of your investment is important. If your venture is pre-product or pre-sales, your strategy is still very fluid. Your ultimate product or service, value proposition, business model, target market, and growth strategy are still to be determined. If a strategic investor finds your prospects interesting, they are making assumptions about your ultimate strategy and how it will mesh with theirs. They might invest in you as an enterprise software company, only to find, by the next financing, that you are now a consumer hardware company. As you can imagine, those changes will cause them to reconsider their continued support.

Second, the strategic investor is called just that because they are looking for investments that further their business strategy. The problem is that *their* strategy is also subject to change. So while you may still be the same enterprise software company you were on the day they invested, their strategy may now call for a consumer hardware partner. You have two unpredictably changing strategies that need to align to get the most out of the relationship.

Moreover, a strategic investor on your capitalization table—or, worse yet, on your board—may spook other companies, like their competitors, from doing business with you. You may find that by cozying up to one partner, you alienate everyone else. This is compounded when looking at a merger or acquisition. Competitive bids may be in short supply if companies feel their rival has an inside lane to acquiring you. Consequently, the value of your company may be capped or discounted once you bring on a strategic investor.

And strategic investors are not reliable follow-on investors. So they can send a very negative signal in subsequent rounds of financing if they choose not to participate.

Often strategic investments are coupled with strategic business agreements. What makes a strategic investor particularly attractive is their ability to bring more than money to the table, providing you with the advantages of their organization, brand, sales channels, and/or customers. While their investment arm may be excited by your venture, however, their business arm may feel threatened or just uninterested. You may find yourself navigating a tricky conflict within your strategic investor, and perhaps never receive the business advantages you believed you were going to get along with their money.

Board meetings with strategic investors present can become complicated, choreographed affairs if you have to exclude their representatives from sensitive discussions, like dealings with their competitors or bids from their rivals. And strategic investors also can be torn between their fiduciary duty to you and their own self-interest.

Needless to say, accepting an investment from a strategic investor brings challenges. They may well be worth it, and there are plenty of examples of strategic investors who make very good partners and even attractive acquirers. But you will need to do your homework and structure the relationship properly from the start.

THE
IDEAL
FUNDRAISE

Part 2 presented rules for selecting the right investor.

In part 3, we share rules for obtaining the "best" funding for your venture. A fundraising strategy is not simply episodic; rather, it should be adjusted and refined based on the stage of your venture, your performance, your industry, macroeconomic factors, and investor sentiment, among other things. Most important, though, your fundraising strategy should be aligned with your venture's business model and its consequent equity, debt, and working capital requirements, as well as limitations. Fundraising is a time sink, and while you are out raising capital, your competitors are out hiring the best talent, winning customers, and gaining critical competitive ground. This part of the book will help you prepare your fundraising so as to minimize the disruption to your venture while maintaining control over the process to produce the best outcome.

Raise capital in stages as you remove risk.

M ost startups raise money throughout their lifetime in discrete stages. You often hear the terms "seed stage," "series
A," "series B," "growth stage," etc. The definitions are always
changing, but they loosely apply to the stage of the company's
development (pre-product, pre-sales, pre-revenue, etc.) and the
amount of money the company is seeking (less earlier and more
later as the burn rate increases). Frankly, the stages indicate as
much about the shifting focus of investors—with angels investing
more in seed-stage ventures and larger venture firms gravitating
to growth stage—as they do about the maturity of your startup.

Why raise money in stages? It's so time-consuming and
anxiety-provoking to raise capital—why not raise all the money
you will ever need right now?

First, if you raise more money than you need in an attempt
to remove the leap-of-faith risks too early, you will pay a
big price. Given everything that you still have to prove and
accomplish, on a risk-adjusted basis, your valuation will be too
low to provide you and your team with a compelling upside
after you absorb all the dilution a "one-and-done" round would
entail. Simply stated, you are too risky at the start to raise all
the capital you need at an attractive price.

Second, and the corollary to the first point, if you use the money you raise at each stage to remove the white-hot risks, then investors will be willing to invest more, at higher prices, in later rounds. This minimizes dilution for you and your team while providing more confidence about how you will spend the money intelligently to create more value.

Third, you are less likely to attract a quality investor for a one-and-done financing than you will if you perform consistently to reduce risk and earn the respect of top-notch investors along the way. You may think all investors are just looking for the lowest price, but in fact they are looking for the best risk-adjusted price for a likely big winner. If an investor does not have some special insight that gives them conviction before you can show results, they will prefer to wait. You will be able to bring more talent around the capitalization table and into the boardroom as your company persistently executes, creating a stronger ecosystem for your success.

Fourth, raising too much money too early can undermine your discipline and lead you off track. Returning to the market every few years for more capital forces you to prioritize your efforts and confronts you with the realities of your business. With the confidence of cash, you may fail to methodically test your assumptions, deliver your technology, demonstrate your product, validate your market, and prove your economics before scaling. Too much money insulates you from vital market feedback, allowing you to ignore the obvious while you persist in the belief that, with more time and effort, you will prove yourself right. Maybe—but it is healthy to have to face the questions at every stage in a visceral way.

Fifth, before there are customers, there are investors. They are the best market feedback you will have until the market can speak for itself. Imperfect as it is, this feedback is invaluable early in your venture, when you are flying on blind intuition. Listening to their responses as you solicit their investment from stage to stage can be helpful input.

There may, in fact, be an advantage in raising more than one stage of capital in a single fundraise when the market is exuberant and investors are willing to forward-price your venture as if the white-hot risks have already been removed. But raising a one-and-done round is not a panacea. The time-tested way to preserve value for you and your stakeholders and to enforce market discipline is by raising money in successive rounds as risks are removed and performance is demonstrated. Remember: in each successive round, your earlier investors are in the same boat as you so long as they are not leading the new round; they want the best investors, the highest price, and the lowest dilution.

A good practice when raising capital in stages is to write a ten-page draft deck for your next fundraise immediately after the close of your current fundraise. This deck is simply a brief summary of the progress you hope to make and the pitch you hope to present when you have spent the capital you just raised. The slide headings tell the story. It will focus you like a laser on the things you need to accomplish and how you plan to spend your time and resources. It also trains your attention on the never-ending task of raising money. So, if you just raised your series A, now is the time to sit down and draft a ten-page deck for your future series B round. This will help identify your critical milestones and clarify any fallbacks you might pursue in case you come up short of the ledge.

Minimizing dilution is not your fundraising objective.

You probably feel tremendous pressure to always deliver higher-funding valuations in each successive round. It has become a point of pride to brag about the value of your company in a private financing. It used to be a point of pride to brag about your profitability and outcomes, but that is another story. It might be worth noting that privately held unicorns do not actually exist, although some investors seem to forget that. Unicorns only become real when they are liquid and you can count the money.

A private-financing valuation is at best indirectly related to the actual or potential value of your venture. It is more directly related to the competitiveness of the financing environment and the hot trends in investing. As in any market, valuations will fluctuate. And because the private-financing market is by its nature small and illiquid, you can expect valuations of private ventures to be very subjective and volatile. Sadly, the effect is often binary, with companies and investing themes being either in favor and attractive or out of favor and nearly unfundable.

So it behooves you to strategize your financing carefully, projecting all the way to cash flow breakeven, the point at which *you* control the business, not some new investor. You are aiming for the higher end of market valuations in each round, calculated to raise sufficient capital to allow you to make enough progress to increase your valuation to the higher end of market in the subsequent round.

If, instead of setting your valuation at a level you feel you can exceed in the next round, you maximize your current valuation around a single, frothy moment in the market and price your round too high, you may well have to adjust your valuation downward in a subsequent round—jeopardizing morale and momentum. There is nothing inherently bad about taking money in a subsequent round at a lower valuation; but the optics, for investors, employees, and customers, can be challenging. You don't want to appear to be damaged goods. And down rounds (a fundraise at a lower valuation than the previous one) have consequences. One of the paragraphs in the term sheet you signed provides for adjusting the price of prior rounds based upon the new, lower valuation. So you suffer twice: more dilution in this round and more dilution retroactively for the prior rounds.

Be sure to anticipate future round pricing and try to value your venture so that your valuation is likely to increase, not decline, even if it means taking a lower valuation today. Don't maximize; optimize, by demonstrating continuing momentum through a series of increasing funding valuations. If you are concerned about dilution, you can raise less money now, at a slightly lower valuation, to equalize for dilution.

If you do decide to take the frothy valuation, consider raising enough money to insulate yourself from having to raise a future down round by creating a buffer and funding more than just the immediate-stage requirements. Perhaps you can even fully fund multiple stages at one time if the terms are sufficiently attractive (and then husband the cash dearly to avoid bloat).

In the interest of preserving bragging rights rather than serving the business, some entrepreneurs try to resolve a disagreement about valuation with deal terms rather than price. It comes down to how each party perceives the risks and potential outcomes. You can address both with ratchets that issue new shares, effectively lowering the price, if you fail to perform to plan. But this is precarious and should be done only as a last resort. It sets a bad precedent for future rounds and misaligns the interests of management and the investors. After all, with the ratchet, your investors will benefit from your failures in the short term; you won't. And if you try and solve the valuation gap by guaranteeing your investors a multiple of their investment to juice their returns, you have created a conflict around liquidity in a certain price range, such that your investors get their multiples, but your employees get nothing.

The right answer is to forgo all the financial engineering and set a fair valuation, even if it is not the maximum available at the time. It is a bit like playing billiards: you want to make the shot in front of you, but you also want to ensure that you set up the next shot while sinking this one. Dilution is only relative; it's running out of cash that is terminal, and you have to be thinking about the next round now.

RULE 44

Don't let a temporary fix become a permanent mistake.

When accepting money from any capital provider, whether an investor, lender, or vendor, you must understand what bells and whistles are attached in order to fully evaluate its "cost" to you. This is especially crucial when you will require multiple rounds of capital. The terms established in the first round will be very hard to eliminate in later rounds. So focus on executing only simple, plain, vanilla structures. If you approach each negotiation tactically rather than as part of a long-term strategic plan, you are likely to create problems for yourself down the line.

One company we know accepted a favorable valuation in exchange for certain voting rights, which effectively gave the investor veto power over certain company decisions, like raising future rounds and achieving liquidity. In later rounds, the company tried to remove the term, but each successive investor in turn insisted on similar threshold voting requirements, which essentially gave them veto power as well. Key decisions were thereby taken out of management's and the board's hands and delivered to the shareholders, creating a messy situation that could have been resolved in the first financing if only the company had accepted a slightly lower valuation without the offending terms.

It is best to negotiate all the controversial business terms

in the term sheet, so as not to be blindsided by additional de-
mands in negotiating the definitive documents, especially since
at that point you will be more vulnerable to a broken financing
and unable to walk away. This applies to both equity and debt
instruments.

And remember: be a wise negotiator. You aren't selling a
car; you are bringing on trusted partners. The negotiation is
about problem solving, not haggling. Know exactly what terms
you need, and don't grind the other ones. Know what terms
your investors need, and try wherever possible to agree to them.
A scorched-earth policy sets the wrong tone for the relationship
and won't net you anything significant. The negotiation is
another opportunity for both parties to evaluate each other's
character, judgment, and chemistry. If you fight over crumbs
no one will ever give you cake.

You are not just solving today's problem; you are setting the
stage for tomorrow's problem. If you start out with unnecessary
complexity, you are stuck with it. Therefore, target capital
providers who share your startup's risk profile and potential,
stakeholders who play to win alongside you and not at your
expense.

Later-stage investors, for instance, who pay more to participate often financially engineer their terms to protect their
downside, rather than align with you for the upside. Their
terms are less likely to be appropriate for an early-stage business. A truly disruptive venture, coupled with a plan requiring limited funding in a hot market, with the potential for an
early, big exit, can pick and choose its investors and terms. All
others need to tread cautiously and negotiate wisely.

Pursue the lowest-cost capital in light of your circumstances.

As your business matures and cash flows become more predictable, your venture can shift from exclusively equity-based financing to include more debt-based financing. But remember that this transition requires high confidence that the cash flows from operations are more than sufficient to service the debt.

Entrepreneurs often think they have landed a windfall when they find someone willing to lend them money without demanding ownership in return. When the payments become due before the revenues start arriving, however, it can be a shock to see your burn rate increase and your cash-out date accelerate at exactly the wrong moment.

While there still is significant execution risk and uncertainty about your cash flows, you should be more conservative and avoid leverage, even when tempted by its perceived lower cost of capital. Selling equity is expensive, but a debt holder will demand certain rights and security that will severely limit your options if things take longer or don't develop as you expect—and they usually don't. If you hit a wall and need to cut back to fight another day, debt service may keep you from being able to slim down to a healthy burn rate.

If you can't cover your debt service out of positive cash flow, your secured loan begins to resemble preferred equity ownership, with the right to demand that you liquidate assets or the company in order to pay them back. This security interest has seniority over your preferred investors, you, and your common shareholders. If you can't make your debt payments when they're due, you have effectively granted a controlling interest to your lender.

Debt works for businesses that can benefit from the associated tax breaks. It is a cheaper source of capital for companies that can confidently afford the debt service. But that is not your situation at the early stage. So it is prudent to minimize debt and limit burdensome leases (longer-term obligations) while focusing on raising equity to fund your business.

RULE 46

Escape the traps of venture debt.

There are many types of debt. There are bank loans, leases, and venture debt, among others. Bank loans are usually reserved for later-stage businesses that have predictable cash flows and profitability. They have relatively low interest rates and favorable terms.

Leases are debt granted in conjunction with the purchase of assets that can serve as security for the loan. The lender may be the vendor, or a third party. The terms are attractive if the assets hold their value and are easily repossessed by the lender in the event of a default, though there are usually down payments and pre-payment and post-payment requirements that can add up. Fortunately for startups, the viability of the lessee is less important than the residual value of the assets.

Venture debt is a specialty loan provided to high-risk startups that aren't yet profitable and may have very limited or nonexistent cash flows. Unlike leases, they can be used to pay for anything. They don't offer the advantages of a security interest in the assets purchased, so the terms can be very expensive. And venture debt lenders often demand a security interest in your intangible gems, like your intellectual property, which will give them oppressive leverage in the event of a default.

The arguments for venture debt seem convincing: (1) it provides more time between equity rounds for extending your runway and achieving higher valuations; (2) it allows the owners to retain larger ownership stakes through lower dilution; and (3) by bringing additional capital earlier, it helps the company achieve milestones, and therefore liquidity, sooner for its investors. It may be used for factoring receivables (e.g., a cash advance for yet uncollected receivables) or financing working capital. It may seem even sweeter if the venture debt postpones any repayments of principal or interest for some time, even if like those "zero down, no payments until next year" car loans, they always come due eventually. In a perfect world, venture debt does have its appeal.

Needless to say, the world is not perfect, and you should preserve the option to pivot, refine course, and adjust milestones in response to the challenges and risks ahead. Venture debt locks you in. With the debt repayment overhang, changes may be impossible, because your investors are only interested in investing in the creation of new value, not paying old debts. At the very least, a venture lender can negotiate for more when you are in distress, because they control the cards.

Some ventures choose to pay the fees and grant the warrants to secure venture debt but then don't actually take the cash down unless they see a clear opportunity for it, such as a bridge to a significant bump in valuation or a cash gap that needs filling. Be careful, however, about accepting a loan with the intention of taking it down later if things get difficult. Loan covenants such as strict material adverse change clauses (so-called MAC clauses, whereby any significant change in your business could result in your lender calling the loan due) or minimum-deposit rules or compensating balance requirements (which require you to keep sufficient money in your account with the lender to meet your debt requirements, effectively tying up the loan proceeds as collateral and netting you nothing) could mean that when you need the money most, you simply don't qualify for it any longer. Caveat emptor.

If, after considering all the risks, you do decide to take venture debt, choose wisely. Terms are usually comparable, but the best terms don't necessarily equate to the best deal. Terms include the interest rate, payment schedule, loan security, warrants to buy your stock at an advantaged price in the future, loan takedown conditions, and funding covenants, among other things. More important, pick a lender with a reputation for working with companies and investors when problems occur to help the business survive rather than to pull the plug—a so-called relationship lender.

In contrast to venture debt, if structured properly, venture leasing could provide a lower cost of capital with limited risk to the venture. Those expensive computers, desks, chairs, and pieces of production equipment can be paid for over time, by lease, rather than today with expensive venture capital.

Choose one of four approaches to determine how much money to raise.

There always seems to be some confusion about just how much money to raise. There are so many variables—valuation, burn rate, critical objectives, time, dilution, etc.—that serve to confound easy analysis. Your investors may have a preference for raising less today in order to remove key risks and raise more later at a higher valuation, while you and your team may want to raise more now to remove the stress and provide you with the reserves you desire to scale more quickly. Luckily, there are four tried-and-true approaches to narrowing down how much you want to raise at each juncture.

MILESTONE-BASED APPROACH

The first approach is the most common. You start by building a financial plan from the bottom up, determining what resources are required, over what period of time, in order to achieve certain predetermined value-accretive milestones that will allow you to raise your next round or achieve positive cash flow. Your milestones drive the exercise. If you are comprehensive, know exactly what you need, and hit the milestones on time, you are in good shape. On the one hand, you may grossly underestimate the time and resources needed. Sh*t happens. This means that no matter what amount of money you calculate, you should add another 10 to 50 percent to account for the unknowns. The earlier your stage, the more buffer is recommended.

Uncertainties, on the other hand, may bias you toward acquiring more resources than are required and bloating your plan unnecessarily. A bloated plan means a higher cash burn, and a higher burn, in turn, reduces your ability to react to unforeseen setbacks (like changes in the macroeconomy, the fundraising environment, or insider sentiment, to name a few). Drawing the right balance is tricky, and a lot of how you resolve this will depend upon your personal appetite for risk and your venture's access to capital. Regardless of the drawbacks, every venture should have a detailed bottom-up cash requirements plan, though obviously stakeholders will need to appreciate that this plan will change with new information over time.

BURN-BASED APPROACH

Another method, and a sanity check on the milestone approach, is the burn-based approach. This requires working the plan effectively from the top down: you determine what you feel is a reasonable monthly burn rate and the amount of time you think you will need to make meaningful progress, and add the amount of time you estimate it will take to raise your next round. Multiply it all together and you have a fundraise amount. This method uses time rather than milestones to gauge progress. It tends to be more applicable to the earliest stage of a venture, like the seed stage.

Most important, when using this method, you need to accurately estimate how long it will take you to raise the next round and be sure to account for any missteps along the way. The time you set will vary depending on market conditions, the amount of your raise, the perception of your opportunity, and your progress—but three to six months is a good guess.

Think of the burn-based process as putting money into two pockets. The right pocket contains your spending money, the money you will invest in achieving results and reducing risk. The left pocket has your bus money home, the amount you will need to keep the lights on while you raise the next round. Be sure to include all expenses in this monthly burn allowance, including salaries and benefits, lease and debt service, fixed costs (rent, utilities), variable costs (marketing and sales), and obviously any external programs and consultants required to complete the tasks.

This approach is all about living within a set budget. It is good discipline for staying lean and mean as an early venture.

RUNWAY APPROACH

A third approach, and a somewhat more fluid, rolling process, is to set a specific target runway period based loosely upon your industry and your stage. Let's say that you are comfortable closing your next round within six months of commencement, and you want no less than six months' worth of working funds at any moment; then you would set a target of twelve months. That means that as your cash approaches the twelve-month level, you swiftly raise more capital to replenish the coffers—

hopefully much more than an additional twelve months' worth. But regardless, you would always endeavor to have at least twelve months' worth of runway in the bank. If your cash falls below the twelve-month point and you still don't have your fingers firmly on the next round, you start cutting costs gradually to extend your runway as needed. This way, you slowly slim the organization instead of falling off a cliff, managing your risks before running out of money.

This approach does, however, require a lot of discipline and intestinal fortitude. Your venture is, in essence, always gradually adjusting the slope of its burn rate as plotted on a graph, trying to never hit the ground. Especially when raising equity is going more slowly than expected, this can be a frustrating strategy to pursue. But it does help the venture to adjust more smoothly to the reality of its situation rather than snapping back spending abruptly at the very end. If you take this approach, be mindful of keeping as many of your operating expenses as possible variable rather than fixed so that you can adjust your spending without disrupting your core activities.

DILUTION APPROACH

Sometimes your fundraise is simply a function of how popular you and your venture are. If you are hot, in a hot industry, investors may throw money at you. If the valuation is high enough, you can solve for dilution rather than for milestones, burn rate, or runway. This analysis is really about how much money to raise beyond what your plan requires, largely because the excess is so "cheap." The focus here is on dilution. Set an amount by which you are willing to dilute in this round, multiply by the rich valuation you are receiving, and raise that much.

For example, if you need $100 and feel that your company is worth $400 (your pre-money valuation, i.e., before adding the amount raised), you would expect to sell 20 percent to raise that amount ($100 divided by $500, your post-money valuation, i.e., after the money raised is added to your pre-money valuation). If someone values you at $800 rather than $400, you could raise $200 with the same resulting 20 percent dilution. In that case, you may decide that 15 percent dilution is your limit and raise only $140. You get the picture.

Now for the tricky part. With the excess money, don't be lulled into bloating your plan. Bank it. Buy more time. Fund more experiments. Accomplish more before you need to raise the next round or get to cash flow breakeven and forgo it entirely. Be smart.

In the milestone-based approach, you set performance constraints. In the burn-based approach, you set monthly burn-rate constraints. In the runway approach, you set time constraints. And in the dilution approach, you solve for dilution. In practice, all of these methods bleed into one another, and you will likely be employing the first three methods, and, if you are blessed, maybe the fourth, to some degree or another during the course of your fundraisings. Be familiar with them and know which one to emphasize under the appropriate circumstances.

Always have your aspirational plan ready.

Present your base plan to investors, but be ready with your aspirational plan if asked. It is not uncommon in overheated markets for well-heeled and aggressive investors to look for ways to invest more, not less. If they like your venture, they may well ask what an additional 25 or 50 or even 100 percent would do for your business. You should be able to show them how more money could amplify or accelerate your success. Ideally raising a little more money now will allow you to achieve your later-year objectives earlier, effectively compressing your four-year plan into three.

This will also help align you and your existing investors with an understanding of the trade-offs between various fundraising scenarios, the commensurate dilution, and potential growth acceleration. Don't confuse this approach with the poor advice that some entrepreneurs and investors will give you to present an overly optimistic, lowball plan to whet the appetite of new investors in the hope that competitive investors will bid up that amount to meet your actual forecasted needs. This is risky, because the lowball number is insufficient for achieving your stated goals and you are betting on competitive market dynamics and oversubscription to get you the true minimum amount of capital required.

Be straight, but smart.

RULE 49

More ventures fail from indigestion than from starvation.

Raising too much money can be a curse. Early ventures with too much cash lose focus and become bloated. Warning: you may think that this will not happen to you . . . but it will. Ventures are a bit like goldfish: feed them too much and they will explode. Despite the classic theory of capital allocation, which predicts that investors will carefully increase their exposure in a venture only with more information, investors are very often willing to provide ventures with too much money, especially in overheated markets. Competition, deal scarcity, and herd behavior all drive investors to chase the same deals.

Ideally, investors should infuse capital in stages as the venture decreases its risks. This allows them to meter their investments as your performance gives them more confidence and, because of your limited resources, it exposes your venture to market stresses that will drive rapid refinement and improvement. One venture we know recently wasted a full year and tens of millions of dollars scaling with non-economic customers (customers who would never spend enough to pay for the cost of acquiring them) because their prodigious fundraise permitted them to ignore their business in the blind pursuit of growth. And this venture is by no means unusual. Too much capital allows you to ignore market feedback, especially negative feedback, and to fail to adjust to reality as it becomes painfully apparent. Moreover, any money and time wasted on a bloated plan reduces the internal rate of return on capital to your venture, even if it doesn't sink it entirely. Remember: while your strategy might change with more cash or less cash, more cash should not justify your abandoning discipline. It is crucial to make every single dollar sweat, every day, throughout your business.

RULE 50

Never stop fundraising.

It is natural, after laboring to raise a round of investment, to want to focus inward on your business and to come up for more "air" again only when you are running out of cash. This is as inefficient as it is risky. Make sure to have an ear to the ground at all times and keep outside investors apprised of your business progress. This will help close your next round a lot faster. Appreciate that investor selection is an active process, and one that evolves as your venture develops. Do not shy away from having informational coffee meetings and sending regular updates even if your next financing is not a concern yet. An investor who passed on you in an early round may well be interested in investing in a later round if, in the interim, you have addressed their biggest risks or they have had a simple change of heart. Actively stay in touch with anyone you have met in your fundraisings who you feel would be a good partner.

Investors know that investing is a relationship game, and it benefits them to get to know you before investing in your venture. It will give them a head start when you begin the fundraising process, or it might even encourage them to preempt your fundraising process with an attractive offer if they like what they hear. When you need additional money, it will be a lot easier to engage the right investors, because (a) you have had the time to verify their sincere interest, conduct background checks, and understand their appetite for an investment at your specific stage and in your industry, at the amount requested, and (b) the investors already know you and your team and have watched your progress. It is the just-in-time cold-call approach that makes raising money so stressful. Seek investors who invest in you and your team, not just your product or service. A solid partnership is best achieved by constantly vetting and pursuing the right investors instead of panicking and entering into a bad relationship when your cash balance dwindles.

RULE 51

Venture capital moves in cycles.

The time to take the hors d'oeuvres is when they are being passed. There may not be another chance, and dinner might not be in the cards. We know that venture capital moves in cycles, yet many entrepreneurs and investors seem to ignore that and stick to their own internal schedules. If the environment is right for funding, go for it, even if you don't need the money yet. If investors are willing to forward-price your round, meaning value you as if you have already achieved your objectives or forecast without regard for the inherent risk in accomplishing them, by all means hear them out.

This does not mean you should gorge on capital with the wrong terms from the wrong investors. It does mean making sure you always have a buffer and obtain capital when it is most readily available. Understanding the fundraising environment means understanding the preferences and approaches of your target investors, as well as their sentiment and strategy in the current cycle.

Don't wait until your plan suggests that it is time to raise money. Rather, have a vetted list of potential candidates at the ready. What kinds of investments do they prefer? Which markets or industries? Which stage of business? Do they add substantive value to the management team, and are they poised under pressure? Do they have a reputation for following through on their promises and closing on their term sheets? Whom do they like to syndicate with? Who will be the lead partner, and how does she or he fit with your venture? Where are they in the life of their fund? Is there follow-on money reserved, or are they near the end of the fund and ready for another raise from their limited partners? Are they bullish, coming off a successful fund, or anxious, coming off a failing one? If you put in the effort, when conditions dictate you will know whom to talk to.

The time is always right for raising money on good terms from the best investors. And, just as cycles start, they also stop, sometimes very abruptly. Investors are motivated by either fear or greed. Fear of missing out—FOMO—can make smart people do dumb things. And a greedy exuberance for the market potential may drive competition. But fear of an impending downturn or greed for aggressive terms may herald the end of an investment cycle. Macro conditions like elections, wars, disasters, and even public market gyrations can suddenly close the door on private capital for pre-revenue companies. So be a bit paranoid and eat up when the trays come by.

RULE 52

Fundraising takes more time than you think.

Allow six months or more (depending on your situation) for a full formal fundraising process, and manage the timeline as closely as possible while dragging your investors along. Investors will not share your sense of urgency. It is to their advantage to always wait until the last minute, because time will bring more information, and more information reduces risk. On the other hand, you don't want one investor to race to a term sheet, because that term sheet will come with an expiration date, and if others aren't ready to respond, you will be forced to make a binary decision without knowing your options.

In every fundraise, twists and turns will occur. The process includes meeting potential investors, presenting at partners' meetings, responding to detailed due diligence requests, and then negotiating and finally closing the definitive agreements. Only then is the money in the bank.

Depending on the funding rhythm and company needs, you may need to allow for two or more closings so that late-comers can complete their due diligence and join the round later. Note that investors who close early are not eager to extend the second closing too long, because time is knowledge, and allowing later investors to invest on the same terms with more knowledge is not strictly kosher.

Between the acceptance of a term sheet and the final closing and wiring of funds, there can easily be six weeks or more of negotiating details, fulfilling regulatory requirements, and so on. It is often during this last bit of the process that surprises arise, jeopardizing the entire funding. In order to be as efficient as possible, it is important to set the right timing expectations among the various parties from the very beginning.

First, start the process in parallel with your target investors so you can herd them to term sheets more or less simultaneously. Don't be forced to accept a first term sheet without knowing whether there is a better option, or to reject a term sheet without knowing there is a second one.

Second, create urgency and scarcity. Let your candidates know that the train has left the station and they have a limited time to board. And while you should always be transparent with them about where you stand, don't share the names of the other investors you are talking to. Venture capitalists know one another, and it's in their interest to share information and drive down valuations or impose terms.

Third, be scrupulous and honest. If you try to bluff an investor and are found out, you will not only lose their participation, but you may well lose your reputation and the chance to bring on *any* bona fide investors. It's a fine line between creating urgency and making false claims. Don't cross it.

Finally, it's not over until the money is in the bank. Don't relax when the term sheet is signed. By signing the term sheet's "no shop" clause—an agreement that, for a specified period, you will not solicit other offers or engage in negotiations with anyone but the other party—you have now put your fate in the hands of a single lead investor. The term sheet is not an enforceable commitment for them to invest; it's a commitment for them to do their due diligence. Until the term sheet expires you have no other options but to negotiate. Be sure to check on the lead investor's reputation for closing on their term sheets. Many venture capitalists use term sheets as options to tie up a deal while they decide what to do. They have few qualms about leaving you high and dry. Don't work with firms like that. While a term sheet may not be a legal commitment to invest, it's an ethical one. Work only with ethical investors.

RULE 53

The pitch must answer the fundamental questions about your venture.

Preparing for the pitch as well as its supporting materials is a great opportunity for you to take a step back and reflect on your business plan and, more important, on your business model. The key to a good pitch and process is to present sufficient details to demonstrate your mastery of your business. View this as an opportunity to bring clarity to your vision and purpose. The pitch should be simple, engaging, comprehensive, and concise—ideally, it should take no more than fifteen to twenty slides to adequately present the crux of your venture. In general, the pitch should aim to cover ten critical topics and address ten crucial questions, tailored, obviously, to the particularities of your specific venture:

1. **VISION AND MISSION:** Describe your vision for success. If they dream the dream with you, what is the exceptional outcome? Why does your venture matter? The key questions for you to answer here are, Why are you passionate about doing this and why should an investor care enough to join you?

2. **PROBLEM:** Present the problem or pain point your venture is solving and how this may have been

addressed by others in the past. It's important to demonstrate the validity of your problem by pointing to existing solutions or unmet demand. You will address how you plan to compete with these solutions later in the pitch. For now, the question to answer is, Why is this a big, important problem worth solving?

3. **SOLUTION AND VALUE PROPOSITION:** Present your solution and show examples of its effectiveness for potential customers. This is where you highlight the unique aspects of your innovation, its improvements over today's solutions, and its ultimate value to customers. The pertinent questions are, Why is your solution compelling to customers, and what is it worth to them?

4. **MARKET OPPORTUNITY:** Present a detailed description of the ideal customer and the aggregate size of the market, including your total addressable market, your beachhead market, and your aspirational share of each. You want to paint a convincing picture of the target customer and then demonstrate that there are crowds of others like them who will demand your product; a huge unmet need that only you can solve while dominating a large and growing share of the market. Be sure to address the channels by which you will be able to reach these customers. The question to answer here is, How big, ripe, and accessible is the market for your product?

5. **CONTEXT AND COMPETITION:** Present the historical

evolution of your target market: your competitors and their respective strengths and weaknesses, as well as what advances your venture's solution offers. Differentiate your solution from your competitors' in terms of the core customer value proposition. If your competition is entrenched, how will you unseat them? If they are also startups, how will you outpace them? And timing is everything. Distinguish others who failed on this road before by pointing out how the situation and landscape have changed. In short, Why is this the right moment for you to succeed and beat the competition?

6. **PRODUCT:** Present the product's unique value and features, including your protectable intellectual property as well as your product development road map. Show how you expect to quickly follow up on your initial solution with successive products and services. Be clear about how your technology will protect your lead and create downstream opportunities for growth. You need to answer the questions, Why will your product disrupt the existing market, and where does it go from here?

7. **UNIT ECONOMICS AND BUSINESS MODEL:** Show your target unit economics, the amount each discrete transaction will contribute to your operating profit. Share your assumptions on pricing, cost of goods, supply chain costs, and your economic value chain. While this is all inexact at this point, you want to master these numbers and be able to answer the key

questions about cost-down curves, scale leverage, etc., paying careful attention to the sensitivity analysis of your assumptions. If you have to spend a dollar to make a dollar, your business is not very compelling. The key question is, Why will this be a profitable and thriving business?

8. **TEAM, LEADERSHIP, AND ORGANIZATION:** Introduce the founders, senior management, board, and advisers, and include your view on any significant gaps in the team and how you plan to address them. It can be helpful to describe in specifics what you are looking for in any additions to your team. If any of your current team is not expected to scale with the business, be frank about it and explain how you will manage the transition. If you feel that you might not be the right CEO at a future stage of the business, discuss that as well. Answer the questions, Why is this the right team to make this venture a huge success, and how will your organization scale over time?

9. **FINANCIALS AND EXECUTION PLAN:** Provide a historical and forward-looking profit-and-loss statement, balance sheet, and cash-flow analysis, sources and uses of capital, your future capital requirements, and your future financing plans. Be sure to forecast out at least three years. Note that the earlier your business stage, the more unreliable your numbers will be. And the further out your plan goes, the less credible it is. Especially if you are still pre-sales. But while your near-term plan should be substantiated bottom-up,

your out years can illustrate the scope of your vision. And the inherent uncertainty does not excuse you from being detailed and analytical about the assumptions you are making and the sensitivities of your results to variations in those assumptions. Investors will discount your plan to account for your optimism, so present the most optimistic plan you can defend. In fact, as already discussed, you should present two plans, with the base plan being a more conservative "line of sight" plan, along with an aspirational plan that illustrates the upside potential. The plans should address the total amount of capital you expect to raise before liquidity so that investors can calculate their expected dilution and commensurate returns. And you might highlight potential returns with market data about the outcomes for similar ventures. These plans are the lingua franca of your business, and they provide the foundational glue for your pitch. They are testimony to how you *think* about your business. The important question here is, Why should investors have confidence in your plans and, as a consequence, everything else you have told them about you and your business?

10. **INVESTMENT OPPORTUNITY:** Outline your funding history (investors, invested dollar amounts, percentage ownership, prior valuations), current capitalization table, and proposed deal structure. Be prepared to discuss the adequacy of your stock option pool to address the additional hires between now

and the next financing. It's best to have a bottom-up analysis to back up your forecast. This can be a bone of contention, because investors want the company to dilute ownership to provide for future hires by increasing the size of the pool before they invest so they don't have to share in that dilution. Be wary of investor rules of thumb as to how large to make the pool. You can do the math—estimate the stock grants associated with your hiring plan to provide a sanity check. The final question you answer here is, Why is your venture going to be a black swan, providing extraordinary returns for your investors?

Too often, entrepreneurs present their plan as primary research for the investors to wade through and arrive at their own conclusions. This is wrongheaded. The presentation is an opportunity to sell your ideas. It's a narrative, a chance for you to tell your story beyond the nuts and bolts of the business. Every slide heading should be a plank in the ultimate conclusion that your venture is destined to succeed and deliver great returns. Every fact should be evidence in support of those assertions. Use declarative statements. Don't waste a word. The headings should tell the whole story, and every bullet on each slide should support its heading assertion. However, don't write out your presentation verbatim in the slides. The slides capture key insights and facts; the details come from you verbally while presenting. The slide deck is the bun; your in-person presentation is the meat.

Make sure to do dry runs of the presentation with existing

investors or trusted advisers for candid feedback before meeting new investors. You get only one chance to make a first impression. The best pitches are clear and convincing and lead to the logical conclusion: you are going to win, and your investors are going to make a lot of money.

RULE 54

Make it personal.

In the stampede toward the bank, it is easy to forget that business is all about people. Your pitch should specifically address three of them: you, your customer, and the investor.

First, it's all about you. Who are you? Why are you doing this venture? Why are you the best person to make this venture succeed? There's no need to deliver a heart-piercing personal narrative—we've both seen some pitches carried to this extreme—but telling your personal story, authentically, can make a big difference. Your venture may boil down to a "big data for farmers" business, but your roots in a small farming community, your high school job distributing boxes of fresh produce for local farmers, and your work after college at Cargill, learning the ropes of Big Agriculture, all paint a compelling picture of why this is important to you personally. Your committed work with local food banks, for instance, demonstrates a passion for solving the problems of real people and adds more than a touch of humanity to your venture's being just another big-data play. Explaining why this is important to you goes a long way toward explaining why it should be important to your investors.

Second, it's about your customers. Who are they? What value are you providing them? Why should we care about their problems? Sometimes entrepreneurs are advised to create "avatars" that represent the characteristics of your target market. But your customers are not just wallets; they are the living and breathing purpose of your venture. Explain that small farmers are very different from Big Agriculture, eking out a modest living on their tiny farms while working two jobs in town to pay the mortgage. Tell investors how underserved these farmers are by the dominant players, which focus on factory farms rather than mom-and-pops. Show how your service will help small farmers to make the best decisions for their businesses, their families, and the environment. Make the investor care whether this customer prospers or withers.

And finally, it's about your investors. Investors see thousands of pitches a year. Most come to them as part of a seemingly random, shotgun approach to finding money. It's the startup version of boiler room cold-calling, with just a bit more sophistication. But an investor wants to know why she or he is the right partner for you, why you chose them specifically. Is it because they have a portfolio in agriculture technology and can bring insights and connections to your business? Is it because they have a reputation for developing leaders and building successful businesses? Is it because you saw them speak at a conference, and their point of view and approach to startups particularly resonated with you? And don't forget to include a slide that specifically asks them for contributions beyond their money. Investors have egos, too, some notoriously large; don't ignore them when making the pitch.

RULE 55

When pitching, carefully read the room.

Make sure to "read the room," arguably one of the hardest things to do during presentations and due diligence. You are nervous, focused on not making a mistake and presenting complicated material. But you still have to pay attention to what is going on around the table. Not only is the quality of your pitch and delivery important, but assessing the body language and carefully listening to the questions raised are critical to understanding each investor's concerns and doubts. After an investor meeting, you should be able to tell whether they are interested in investing based on their level of engagement and reactions.

Avoid overloading the audience with information. While you know your business cold, for them it may be the first time they ever thought about these topics. Reading the room will allow you to determine how best to follow up and address each investor's particular due diligence hurdles. Remember: investors like to think you are addressing them personally, not that they are simply one of a number of random pitches as you troll for money.

The questions asked and the recurring topics discussed reveal key concerns, worries, and assumptions that the investors may uniquely have based upon their prior experience, the experience that forms the lens through which they will evaluate your opportunity. Whatever you do, address their questions honestly and directly, even if it means asking for time to consider their requests so you can get back to them later. The pitch is not just an opportunity to communicate information, but also a rare chance to build trust and demonstrate mastery. To be clear: it's not just your business they are evaluating—it's you.

RULE 56

Use white papers for deep-dive follow-ups.

P articularly if you are covering new ground or working with state-of-the-art technology, a series of white papers can be helpful during the due diligence process, to further the investor's understanding of the more complicated aspects of your technology, product, or business. Note that these should be prepared in advance so that they can be provided at the end of your presentation or as immediate follow-up.

Try not to bog down your pitch with distracting discussions about esoterica. Often, one or more partners in the room will have specialized knowledge or interest and will ask questions that can take your presentation down a rabbit hole. Resist, and offer to address their interests later or off-line. Provide them with the appropriate white paper, or prepare one and send it if you have not anticipated their questions. Whatever you do, don't bore the rest of the room with arcane explanations and risk failing to get through your presentation and making your key points.

Unlike an informational memorandum, used traditionally in the investment banking process, these white papers are stand-alone documents focused on specific topics of interest. Topics may include the details of your technology or product, descriptions of your customers and markets, specifics of your business model or unit economics, expected outcomes, or a more detailed financial model with commentary on the validity of all of your assumptions. Experience suggests that targeting a white paper for each deep-dive topic is often a better strategy than an extended opus, as different investors will have different areas of interest. By reserving deep dives for the white papers, you can focus during the presentation on the key points you need to communicate and on answering the more fundamental questions.

RULE 57

Prepare your financing documents ahead of time.

Prepare the suite of closing documents (financial and legal) ahead of time, to facilitate the final due-diligence-and-closing process. First, make sure to include with your scenario planning a presentable (and thoroughly vetted) financial business model, in spreadsheet form, for use by the investor. This will help them better understand your thinking. If you provide a clean and effective model that has been prepared in advance, this will become the prevailing model of record throughout the fundraise and will allow you to maintain control of the sensitivity analysis and business assumptions.

You should also prepare the binder of legal documents for the closing. Instead of waiting for a term sheet, have one ready to provide to interested investors. And if this is not the first financing round, be sure to supply the prior round's term sheet and closing documents as well. This reinforces how important the specific closing terms of your prior rounds are, because these are likely to become the basis of future-round negotiations.

Also prepare a data room where the investors and their own attorneys can review your historical documents, as well as financials, important legal contracts, market studies, etc. Back in the day, these were actual rooms full of binders, but today they are secure digital destinations. Make sure you issue separate passwords so you can verify who is looking at which materials and for how long, especially with multiple investors potentially visiting the data room at the same time. This tracking information provides insights about where each investor is in their process, what each investor's concerns might be, and where you can augment your information to help them along. Often, visits to the data room spike right after an investor's internal partner update meeting, and this information can provide you with an indication of the topics that have been discussed at the meeting, as well as the questions the partnership might be wrestling with. Investors will weigh risk differently, so learning about their concerns through their data-room activities is a valuable tool in bringing the fundraise to a successful close.

RULE 58

Obsessively drive to the close.

Being respectful and considerate of the investor's concerns does not excuse you from being relentless about how you spend your time getting to the close. Investors are born with FOMO (fear of missing out) and will freely accept pitches or even engage in due diligence for market intelligence purposes rather than for investment purposes, especially if the investor has already invested in a competing venture. What better way to check up on their existing investment than to evaluate what other smart people are thinking about the field?

This doesn't mean investors will necessarily pass your information on to your competition, but they will certainly educate themselves, and their judgment may be influenced accordingly, such that your information can be leaked to your competitor by osmosis.

Do not hesitate to cut the tire-kicker investors out of the process quickly, because your time (and your team's time) is your most valuable resource. Your efforts are much better spent cultivating a number of potential lead investors rather than pursuing your favorite lead who will never get to the close. A common trait of a successful fundraiser is the uncanny ability to know when to let go of certain investors in order to focus time on the ones who have the conviction, money, and willingness to close by the required deadline.

It will take persistence and discipline to close the financing on time. You can't exhale until the cash is in the bank. Run the process the same way you would run your engineering schedule or a product launch. Be obsessed.

RULE 59

Consistent communication is important in convincing investors.

Occasionally, the wheels come off during a fundraising due to inconsistent communication, crossed signals, or mixed messages. It is very important that you clearly articulate to potential investors your mission and vision for success, as well as provide an overarching explanation of what you are looking to achieve in the near, middle, and long term. The message can change over time as your venture evolves between successive fundraises, but it should be ironclad during any single raise. If messages vary too much during investor discussions, or if your progress stalls or reverses, it severely jeopardizes the round.

During the raise, the investors are looking to understand your business, its risks, its opportunities, and your economics. Investors may feel that a venture whose story is changing midstream might still be too early and in too much flux for them to risk an investment. This does not mean that you are required to have all the answers; there is obviously more uncertainty than certainty in an early-stage venture. But ensuring that the plan of record is consistent throughout the various investor presentations for the period of the fundraising will increase your chances of success. Inconsistent messages, bad news, or disappointments during a raise can quickly derail the funding process.

Remember: you need the money, but they don't need to invest—there is always another venture waiting in their lobby. In venture capital, you cannot be "called out on strikes"— which, for all you non–baseball fans, means investors can't fail just sitting on their wallets waiting for the right venture to come along—but they *can* strike out swinging if they back the wrong venture. Also, remember that investors talk to one another and compare notes. If there are discrepancies in your communications among them, they will notice. It therefore also goes without saying that you should never share your investor candidate lists with other investors or they may become conspirators rather than competitors for your deal.

And whatever you do, don't risk disappointing your new investors by missing your numbers or failing to deliver on expectations. The fundraising will take time, and if you have provided a plan that forecasts certain accomplishments or metrics during the fundraising, you'd better achieve them. If not, your credibility is blown. Likewise, be sure that you are not going to go off course immediately after closing a round. Your plan established short- and long-term expectations; be especially sure you can meet your short-term ones. Buyers' remorse can be an ugly thing.

RULE 60

Milestones can solve irreconcilable valuation differences.

Sometimes it makes sense to provide for predetermined investment milestone payments, or "tranches," in the term sheet; these are investment installments to be paid as key milestones are met. This can be an elegant solution when valuation differences between management and investors due to different perceptions of risk can be identified objectively and tied to measurable accomplishments—like shipping your product or achieving certain sales results.

But there are two reasons why this arrangement might not benefit you. First, by the time the milestone is achieved, the investor might have other concerns that make them reluctant to fund the milestone. These milestone tranches are seldom ironclad, and there is usually a way out for the investor. Second, your performance milestones are merely best-guess targets and not foregone conclusions. If you want to pivot or reprioritize certain milestones, you may find the tranche milestones are no longer relevant and impossible to achieve, thereby jeopardizing your future payments. This is especially true if the investor is not on board with the changes you are making.

When possible, you should try to solve the risk problem

at its heart: the valuation. If there is a price that balances the risks, then both sides should feel comfortable. But if not, and if you can distill the valuation debate to a few, very measurable events, then a tranched financing may be a workable solution.

RULE 61

Liquidation preferences will change your outcome.

You might be surprised to learn how few ventures create real wealth for their stakeholders, resulting in squandered career opportunities for you and all of your employees. This can be the case even when the venture is sold at a profit. Given the special liquidity preferences (the right to receive the first money to repay their investment) attached to the preferred stock you sell to your investors, you must understand how the liquidity waterfall works.

Driving up your valuation unnecessarily can be detrimental to employees when seen in the light of liquidity. You and your employees have common shares without preferences. This is largely for pricing and tax purposes; it differentiates between the higher price of the preferred shares you sell to investors and the lower price of the common shares and options you and your team hold so as not to trigger tax obligations for you. But the other side of the coin is that your investors will get their money back, or some multiple of that amount, before any of you will see a dime. The inclusion of caps, multiples, and priorities in structuring liquidation preferences can "reallocate the pie" such that the proceeds of an exit event are distributed very differently than the as-converted fully diluted (taking into account all shares, warrants, and options) ownership percentages would imply. Therefore, pay careful attention to how liquidation preferences are structured when negotiating the terms of a financing. Depending on the terms, there might be greater room for misalignment of interests between preferred and common stockholders in evaluating certain acquisition offers.

But first, bear with us for a moment while we get a couple of details straight. The two most common forms of preferred stock are "participating" and "nonparticipating."

Participating preferred refers to the fact that in the event of liquidity, investors will first receive the amount of their investment (or a multiple of it, as we'll explain later) and then share, pro rata, with the common shareholders in any excess. Nonparticipating preferred, however, gives the investor the right to receive only the amount of their investment, as downside protection. To participate in any excess, they must convert their preferred stock to common stock and share pro rata with the common stockholders in the entire proceeds.

Nonparticipating preferred is generally the choice of common shareholders, while participating preferred is the choice of preferred investors. But nonparticipating preferred does create a complication for common shareholders. This is known as the "dead zone," and it's the price range where the preferred investors have recovered their liquidity preference but are indifferent to a higher price that is insufficient to render their pro-rata slice, after conversion, greater than their liquidity preference. The common shareholders would benefit from a higher price in this zone because they would be entitled to the entire excess, effectively "catching up" with the preferred's take. But because the preferred shareholders see no benefit until the stock price exceeds the dead zone upper limit, they have no motivation to negotiate with the buyer for a higher valuation within that range. Once the common stock price exceeds the dead zone upper limit, the parties are once again aligned in negotiating a higher valuation.

For example, if the preferred investors have invested $1,000 for 80 percent of your venture, and you have an offer to sell your company for $900, they will receive the entire $900 and you will get nothing. If the offer is for $1,500, your preferred shareholders will get their $1,000 back and then some. The "some" depends upon whether they own participating preferred shares; if they do, then you and they split the remaining $500 according to your ownership percentages, 20/80. If they own nonparticipating preferred shares, you would get to "catch up" out of the excess $500 to the amount where your total returns and your investors' total returns actually represent your fully diluted ownership percentages (20/80), after which your investors would convert to common and you both would share the entire proceeds pro rata.

This sounds complicated, and it is. In the above $1,500 example, with participating preferred stock, the investors receive the first $1,000, and you and they split the remaining $500, 20/80—$100 for you and $400 for them, for a total of $100 for you and $1,400 for them. If they own nonparticipating preferred stock, the investors have the right to the first $1,000 and you have the right to the entire excess ($500) unless they convert to common, which they inevitably would because 80 percent of $1,500 is greater than 100 percent of $1,000.

After conversion you both share pro rata in the entire $1,500, resulting in $300 for you and $1,200 for them. The problem is that nonparticipating preferred investors will be indifferent to any valuation between $1,000 and $1,250, the price at which their pro-rata share is equal to their liquidity preference, at which point your investors would convert to common and participate pro rata in the total. Thus there is a dead zone in valuations between $1,000 and $1,250. This conflict can lead to strange results. Add some zeros and the difference can really add up.

The type of liquidation protection provided in your deal will therefore have a meaningful impact on how different investors react to specific exit opportunities. Be especially wary of multiple liquidation preferences, like "2×" or "3×," where investors receive a multiple of their investment back before common holders receive their first dollar. An otherwise seemingly successful outcome may return nothing to the common shareholders if the preferred shareholders receive their multiple first. In the example above, if the preferred shareholders had a 2× preference, they would be entitled to $2,000 before you received a nickel, and even the profitable $1,500 offer would be worthless to you.

Good investors are acutely aware of the misalignment of interests at valuations lower than the dead zone's upper limit. In order to reward you and your team and motivate you to cooperate with a sale at a lower price, at the time of the sale good investors will often create a "pool" for the common shareholders, typically 8 to 10 percent of the total proceeds. Though still less than your pro-rata share, the pool helps unite the interests of the preferred and common holders. Independent expert advice from skilled outside counsel is very important. Understand what is "out of market" (not the norm) in your existing investment climate and negotiate hard to limit the "dead zone."

RULE 62

Do not take rejection personally.

M ost people dread fundraising, because they dread the inevitable rejections. Let go of that part of your ego. Rejection is nothing personal (something to remember when you are pitching publishers on your book). Whether investors do or do not invest in your venture often has little to do with you personally, but rather with the fit between their investment theses, the state of their portfolio, and your venture stage or industry.

Fundraising is like any other form of matchmaking—it is about finding the right match and not just about you. The investor simply might not be interested in your mission or vision, and, frankly, you want to weed out such prospects early. Or they may be finishing up an existing fund and in the process of raising their next one, and you might get more attention from them in a succeeding round. Don't expect every investor to "get it" or care about what you care about. All entrepreneurs have gone through this before. Not landing a particular target investor is sometimes a wonderful stroke of luck. You want a good match.

By taking rejection in stride, you also preserve the relationships you have built during the fundraising process. While the investor may be passing today, they might be interested next time around. Listen to the reasons they give for passing and take note. As you address each in turn, you can let them know and whet their appetite for the next opportunity to invest.

A word about the reasons investors give for passing: they are often misleading. You will hear about your business being at too early or too late a stage. You will hear about your technology or product needing more proof. You will hear about your team being incomplete. You will hear about their being swamped and not having the time to do due diligence. You will hear about customer references that were promising but not yet commitments. In short, you will hear a lot of excuses but seldom the real reasons. Most often, while genuine, these justifications arise because when all is said and done, the investor simply lacks conviction. They may be intrigued but not impressed enough to take the bet. The same excuses can easily be spun into justifications for investing if the investor sees the glass as half full. That is your job: getting the investor emotionally excited. Let them line up the reasons why, rather than why not.

One more caveat: if you are hearing the same concerns echoed by investor after investor, you might want to rethink things. Your first "customers" are actually your investors, so listen to their input the way you will listen to your ultimate users down the road, and course-correct as necessary. If you can, arrange to have your existing lead investor contact potential new investors after you have met with them, in order to collect candid feedback. Done properly, this can help you figure out which parts of your pitch and process are working and which parts aren't so you can fix it.

BUILDING AND MANAGING EFFECTIVE BOARDS

The rules in part 3 focused on obtaining capital and finding the right investors.

The rules in part 4 will help you identify and assemble the right board of directors as well as coach you on how to run an effective board meeting. Given that many investors ask for a board seat as part of their investment, funding and board selection most often go hand in hand and require serious consideration. We have experienced both good and bad boards, from both the management side and the investor side. We have the experience of having been CEO, CFO, the lead investor, the lead director, and the board coach. When you fully understand the various perspectives, the path to creating a functional and effective board becomes clear.

Boards are deliberative bodies, not collections of individuals.

To be bold, startups need good entrepreneurial leadership. Through your venture, you strive to serve and satisfy your various stakeholders, building sustainable value for the long term. Nonetheless, many factors can derail your ambitions, and boards of directors play a unique and critical guiding role in supporting you. A great board is an invaluable asset. They augment your experience, network, and judgment. They can make a big difference in your ability to surmount challenges and create the largest potential. A bad board can sink a good company.

Through their decisions, boards have the power to protect and sustain a venture's core values and mission, but they most certainly also have the ability to destroy those values and mission—unintentionally or otherwise. So when choosing such important partners, never assemble the "cheapest" board, in the form of investors simply willing to invest the most at the highest valuation. After all, you wouldn't hire the cheapest brain surgeon; you want the best brain trust around, and you know that exceptional performance outweighs their nominal cost. Be selective. You get what you pay for.

Once you have assembled a great board, you need to

get the most out of it. If you treat them like your judge and confessors, they will be your judge and confessors. If you treat them like partners, they will be your partners. Unlike other functions in your organization, directors should be most effective operating as a group. Don't make a practice of lobbying or polling them individually; you will only get contradictory opinions and individual perspectives.

Experienced directors are skilled in working as a team. At their best, they listen more than they speak, and they debate and challenge respectfully, realizing their job is to stimulate and test your thinking and evaluate your processes rather than to substitute their judgment for yours. Learn to facilitate the board discussions to tease out a variety of perspectives. Create space in the board meetings for the directors to challenge you and one another so that their ideas can be polished by the group as a whole. And don't expect consensus. Encourage constructive disagreement so you can consider all sides of the issues before arriving at your conclusions. A poorly facilitated board is a chore and even a potential threat to your venture, but an engaged board can be a valuable asset.

RULE 64

Conflicts of interest and conflicting interests are elephants in the room.

It has been said, "No conflict, no interest." Meaning that almost every opportunity worth pursuing will present a conflict of interest. Make sure to identify, anticipate, and manage those conflicts. A conflict of interest arises when a party has two or more competing interests, financial or otherwise, that could possibly corrupt their motivation or decision making. Conflicting interests occur in the general course of business when the parties around the table have different incentives and outcomes.

Every investor who sits on your board wears two hats: they represent their fund or themselves as a shareholder, and they have a fiduciary duty to represent the company as a director. A fiduciary interest is a legal obligation of trust on behalf of another. It is not unusual for the board to vote on issues that may be in the best interest of your venture but not in their best interest as a shareholder, and vice versa. It is critical that each board member recognize these conflicts and that they always vote in the best interests of the company when acting in their role as a director. It is not uncommon for that same director to then vote the exact opposite way as a shareholder. As the CEO and also the representative of the common shareholders, if you are in the board seat, you have a similar conflict of interest.

The board should call out these conflicts of interest when they arise and remind the parties of their roles as directors of the company. How they vote as shareholders is their own concern. If they do in fact fall prey to the conflict and vote against the best interests of the company and in their personal self-interest, they are subject to legal action by the company and other shareholders. Majority shareholders—shareholders whose ownership stake is sufficient for them to outvote the remaining minority shareholders—have particular responsibilities to the minority shareholders by law.

Here are some examples of conflicts of interest:

The company is running out of money and has a very tough term sheet from another inside investor that will materially dilute the common shareholders but is certain to close. (These are sometimes referred to as "cram-down" rounds, because they crush the ownership of the common shareholders.) The company also has a slightly more favorable competing term sheet from an outside investor who has not yet performed due diligence and may not close. You have the opportunity to invest with your fellow insider to preserve your ownership on their cram-down terms, but you don't have the opportunity to invest in the competing term sheet to protect yourself. As an investor, do you vote for the cram-down? As a director, do you vote to take the competing term sheet that is more favorable to the common shareholders?

The company has an offer to sell at a price that will recover all of your paid-in capital but will leave nothing for the common shareholders. The alternative is to raise money, but at a large discount from the prior round, resulting in massive dilution to the existing shareholders but affording the company a chance to continue operations and hopefully build even more value during the next two years. As an investor, do you vote to recover your capital? As a director, do you vote to roll the dice on creating more value than the preferences?

The company has a very attractive offer of acquisition that will result in a good outcome for all the shareholders. But the acquirer has also offered management, including you as CEO, a side deal to pay them to be retained by the acquirer for an additional year in an amount that effectively doubles the valuation of what they are paying other shareholders. Further negotiations might result in a higher valuation for all the shareholders but a smaller retention amount for management, potentially resulting in some employees leaving. As CEO, do you vote for the deal that will give you a disproportionate payout? As a shareholder, do you vote to continue negotiating to trade off management retention for a larger share price for all the shareholders?

As you can see, these can be very thorny issues. You have to be clear on what your conflicts are and be resolute in exercising your fiduciary duty on behalf of the company. What you do as a shareholder or as management to maximize your personal interests is another story.

In addition to conflicts of interest, there are more than a few conflicting interests among investors, between you and the board, or even within the management team. These conflicts are not internal to each party; they arise between parties. Make sure to identify potential conflicting interests early so you can steer around them, or at least anticipate when they may become an issue. Aligning interests is critical wherever possible.

For instance, consider stock options. This is why they were created in the first place: not as just another perk but as a way to align interests between management and the owners. One of the reasons it is common to grant stock options to every employee, including the receptionist, is to align interests. The reason board members are granted stock options and not just paid cash is to align interests.

A common impression is that early-stage investors think like entrepreneurs and structure their investments for the upside. Later-stage investors think like bankers and structure their investments for the downside. Regardless, do your homework and know what type of investor you are working with. A clean term sheet—one without excessive preferences or multiples for investors, and without ratchets or adjustments to price based upon your performance—is a good indicator that you are working with an aligned investor.

Here are some examples of conflicting interests:

The company has an offer to sell at a price that returns a profit to early shareholders, who paid less for their shares, but will not return capital to later investors, who paid more. Do you accept the offer?

The company is prepared to go public, resulting in an impressive return to investors and a payday for management. At the last minute, the stock market declines and the bankers tell you that the opening price will be below a ratchet price that the last round's investors negotiated when they invested. The ratchet effectively means that they will be issued additional shares at no cost in order to increase their returns, but this will dilute you as an early investor. You expect, but can't be certain, that the market will recover shortly and produce a windfall for the later investors. Do you block the IPO or take the sure route to accessing cheaper public market capital now?

The company receives an attractive offer to sell. As the founder, you have a contractual right to have all your shares vested upon a change in control, resulting in being paid in one year what you otherwise would have had to earn over four years. The rest of your team does not have that acceleration provision and will have to work for the acquirer for four more years to receive their full payout. Do you vote for the acquisition and receive a full vesting of your shares? Even if it creates a rift between you and your team? Do you forfeit your acceleration to align your interests with the rest of your team's?

Make a habit of calling out the elephants in the room, whether they are conflicts of interest or conflicting interests. If you expose them and discuss them, they transform from ethical issues to business issues. Business issues are much easier to constructively address.

Your board should be operational rather than administrative.

Governance is for governments. That is not you—you are a startup. You want businesspeople, not bureaucrats. You want a board of strategic thinkers with strong operating backgrounds, who are willing to work hard to make your venture a success. Don't let your board become mere administrators rather than active advisers. Figure out how best to include them wherever they can help you and your venture most. They need to be informed, available, knowledgeable, and engaged. If board meetings are becoming reporting exercises, you are well on your way to establishing a board of governors, not a board of directors. Use their time well and expose your business and team to them. Include the board in working sessions and committee meetings with your team. Ask the members of the board to speak at company meetings or participate in question-and-answer sessions. Be transparent. Share your deepest concerns and most daunting challenges in regular closed sessions at the board meetings where confidences are observed. Allow for one or more strategic discussions at each board meeting, so you can tap their collective wisdom. But most of all, seek their help and work them like rented mules. Admittedly boards have certain governance duties, but they should provide you with a lot more than just oversight.

RULE 66

Small boards are better than big ones.

Big boards regress to the mean. This is the same as managing by committee, a disaster waiting to happen. The key is to have a small, effective board, ideally with one or more independent directors. Being small further underscores the importance of the right qualifications for each individual member. For early-stage startups with at least two rounds of investment, experience suggests that five directors make for a good board. Three is too small, except in the very earliest days, and seven or more becomes a management chore and can be unproductive. You want an odd number to avoid ties.

Here is a suggested board composition for an early-stage venture: two directors, one each representing the lead preferred shareholders, plus seats for you as the CEO and for two independent directors, one of whom hopefully can be a capable coach to you. In the event that you can't find two strong independent directors, consider adding one more director from management (a co-founder might be a good option) to represent the common shareholders.

It goes without saying that if your goal is to convene a small and effective group, you generally don't want to grant attendance rights to board observers. Observers are people who attend your board meetings but are not officially on the board and do not have the same responsibilities and duties as your directors. They don't get a vote. Investors—especially syndicate investors, rather than lead investors—often ask for observer rights when they are not able to secure a board seat or when they wish to participate without formal responsibilities. In either case, and no matter how qualified the person may be, they crowd the room and alter the chemistry and collegiality of the board.

There may be situations where the observer role is an accommodation to an investor whom you don't want as a board member but who is willing to appoint a more qualified director in their stead, though these instances are rare. If you can't eliminate observer rights, the observer should understand that they may be asked to leave portions of the board meeting during sensitive discussions. After all, they don't have the same fiduciary duties as your board members do, and, particularly for strategic corporate investors, they may also have a conflict.

It is important to distinguish board observer rights from simply inviting non-directors to attend all or part of a meeting. Board observer rights give an investor the legal right to attend your meetings and receive board materials. Technically, they are there to observe, not participate, but it's hard to find an investor who can sit quietly for two or three hours. Contrast this with experts or other resources you may invite to attend all or part of your board meetings because they add particular value to the group or a discussion. Also, granting board observer rights is different from allowing one of your board members to occasionally bring an associate to quietly observe and learn so they can support your company better.

The role of a good board is to challenge the team with candid feedback and advice, and this only becomes more awkward and difficult as the size of the room grows, with diverse interests and varying levels of engagement. In the end, the relationship between the management team and the board should be intimate enough to allow for some tough love—full support married with accountability. This is best accomplished in a small setting of committed board members who can develop the mutual trust and respect needed to perform the job well.

Remember: this isn't a party, and you aren't fooling around. This is your board meeting. If there isn't a heck of a good reason for someone to be there—if they won't add significant value to your venture—they don't belong in the room.

RULE 67

Lead investors ask for board seats; qualify them first.

Lead investors usually request a board seat as part of their investment. You might expect that they would want to look after their investment, given the amount of blind risk they are taking with you and your venture. But boards play an important role in your success or failure, and with precious few seats to give out, you want to assure yourself that you are not just getting a good investor, but also a good and productive board member.

Just because they invest does not mean that (a) they know how to be a good director or (b) they can help add value to improve your probability of success. You owe it to yourself to do due diligence on the investor by talking to companies where they serve or have served in the past. Ask about their judgment and expertise. Ask how they interact with other board members and participate as a member of a group. Ask about their work ethic and commitment. Assure yourself that they will bring value, not just oversight, to you and your team.

If an investor insists on a board seat as part of their investment and you feel they are unqualified as a board member, you can simply choose to decline their money. Sometimes you can persuade a good investor to let an industry leader take their place on the board, one who can add more immediate value. You want both the best investors and the best directors; don't make unwise trade-offs you will regret later.

You need a lead director.

The lead director should command the respect of the other directors and of management. She or he should be able to coach the CEO from experience. The lead director should be able to facilitate frank discussions among the directors, in closed sessions and without management, at the end of each board meeting to gather their feedback for the CEO. These should not become political cabals, but be conducted in a spirit of open dialogue among directors, and in the best interests of the venture and the CEO. If you sense intrigue among the board members, you need a new lead director. Following the closed session, the lead director should debrief the CEO without divulging specific confidences from the board conversation. This debriefing is not a substitute for a performance review; rather, it is a session to ensure that everyone is still on the same page and that the CEO has the benefit of the opinions of the directors, as distilled, skillfully, by the lead director.

The lead director creates the conditions for overall board and individual director effectiveness. He or she should demonstrate the highest standards of integrity and probity and set clear expectations concerning the board's behaviors, style, and tone of discussions. They should ensure that everyone's opinions are heard, including the quieter board members, and that all concerns are discussed. They should be responsible for coordinating regular performance reviews of the directors and the CEO and communicate and act upon any action items coming out of such reviews (like replacing a director). The lead director is the facilitator in chief and the director the CEO can lean on to handle sensitive board dynamics.

If you are fortunate enough to have two or more people qualified to lead the board, you can change lead directors every two years or so to balance the responsibilities. If you don't have a lead director and are experiencing difficulties getting the most out of your board, consider appointing one of your directors as the lead, and work with that person to achieve the level of performance you deserve from your board.

RULE 69

Add independent board members for expertise and objectivity.

Independent board members are directors who do not have a material relationship, financial or otherwise, with your company. Investors and management obviously don't qualify. Independents are critical in making decisions where investors and/or management may have conflicts of interest or otherwise demonstrate significant biases. In extreme cases, the entire board other than your independent members may be disqualified from participating in a controversial decision, like whether or not to accept an insider term sheet with terms that favor the investors over the common shareholders.

Day to day, independent board members offer something just as valuable: independent thinking. They should be the epitome of fair and reasonable. They should conduct themselves as unbiased arbiters of the truth and act in the best interests of the company. Ideally, they bring experience and expertise that is lacking but crucial for the success of your venture. And if the chemistry is right, they can also serve as coaches and mentors to you and your team.

Given their personal experience, independent board members should help to keep you and your team on your toes by providing peripheral vision on issues outside of your focus and stimulating your thinking on anticipated issues before they become problems. Choose independent members who are good team players, and avoid people whose success or power leads to domineering behavior. After all, being a good board member is largely about contributing to the team experience. Be sure they have the time to spend on your venture; sitting CEOs, for instance, may make poor independent board members because they have little attention to spare.

If you choose independent directors primarily because they bring much-needed expertise to your company, make sure they also have enduring leadership capabilities and great judgment, or be prepared to swap them out later as your need for their expertise wanes.

RULE 70

True board diversity is a competitive advantage.

D iversity reportedly produces better business results, to say nothing about the social and cultural advantages. Diversity in board composition broadens your perspective and is a safeguard against groupthink. It sets an example for your employees and encourages their diversity as well.

In very interesting research conducted by Harvard Business School professor Paul Gompers, called "The Cost of Friendship," he shows that venture capitalists have a strong tendency to team up with other VCs whose ethnic and educational backgrounds are similar to their own. Unfortunately, that tendency turns out to be bad for business. The more affinity there is between two VCs who co-invest in a new company, the less likely it is that the company will succeed. Gompers found that the probability of success decreased by 17 percent if two co-investors had previously worked at the same company—even if they hadn't worked there at the same time. In cases where investors had attended the same undergraduate school, the success rate dropped by 19 percent. And, overall, investors who came from the same ethnic background were 20 percent less successful than investors with different ethnic backgrounds. "Clubbiness" does not make for an effective board. As an entrepreneur building your board, you have the opportunity to be a great equalizer while strengthening your results.

In selecting a board member, nothing matters more than their demonstrated qualifications to do the job well and add value. But there will be more than one candidate who meets those criteria, and if you can bolster your board with diversity in the selection process, you have benefited twice.

To build a diverse board, you may want to consider employing the Rooney Rule. Dan Rooney was the former owner of the Pittsburgh Steelers football team. He required that his management consider minority candidates for head coaching jobs. To that end, recruiters were always asked to provide a slate of diverse candidates, not just the likely suspects. He did not impose a quota or give minority candidates an unfair advantage; he simply wanted to interview more diverse candidates. If you feel that you are not seeing enough diversity in your candidates, you should direct your recruiters to actively seek more minority candidates for your consideration.

Independent directors offer the opportunity to add diversity to your board, because they don't necessarily reflect the predominantly white male complexion of the traditional investment community. So prioritize diversity, among all their other important qualifications, in selecting your independent directors.

Diversity does not just mean more women or people of color, or people who may have a disability or a different gender orientation. It can mean people with varying socioeconomic backgrounds or international perspectives. Your board may benefit from a mix of younger and older directors. And don't stop there—make sure you get the most from board diversity by giving voice to all views on the board and making sure everyone is heard. Call on people if need be, but don't let them be uncomfortably silent.

———————————

Each director must commit to spending meaningful time.

An effective director should spend significant time working with you and the venture—not just attending meetings, but also communicating and meeting with your team between meetings. On average, high-performing directors spend twice as much time as those who have lower impact, totaling well over forty days a year. Moreover, they also spend extra workdays on performance management, merger-and-acquisition considerations, organizational health, and risk management.

A board seat is a serious commitment and should be viewed as such. This is not just a networking or career event. Make sure your board members understand your expectations and commit to fulfilling them. You may be inclined to populate your board with other like-minded CEOs, but hardworking CEOs usually have insufficient time and attention for another venture. You are exhibit A. Instead consider recently retired executives, executives other than CEOs who are taking on a single outside board role, or accomplished professional directors who can dedicate the attention you need. Choose investors and board members who have a reputation for working hard for their ventures. We have seen both ends of this spectrum, and, to be sure, there are dedicated, hardworking investors and board members alike who go the extra mile to help their ventures. It's also true, however, that many directors are looking to fund their lifestyles with multiple board fees. Regardless of their résumés, if they are not going to do real work to help your venture succeed, to help you build an amazing company and solve tough problems, find someone else.

On the other hand, be sure not to burn your board members out. If you and your team are constantly calling and meeting with directors, you may find that they pull back or resign, especially the ones with full-time jobs. It's a fine balance, and you should err in favor of asking more than less, but be respectful of their other responsibilities.

Board members should come to meetings fully prepared. They should have reviewed all materials beforehand (be sure to get them materials a few days ahead of meetings to give them adequate time), and they should arrive with well-considered questions and discussion points. If you and your lead director are doing your jobs, crucial questions will be shared in advance so you and the board are ready to intelligently discuss them. The board meeting is for deliberation, discussion, and decision making, not a time to rehash materials and metrics that can be reviewed earlier.

RULE 72

Review director performance regularly.

Just like your management team, board members need to be reviewed for their performance and fit regularly, and even reevaluated for their seat periodically to ensure they are engaged and adding meaningful value. Great leaders and individual performers might not be good board members. Given their stature, it can be a delicate matter to deliver a poor performance review to a director, and even harder to ask them to resign. But you deserve a well-performing board, just as you deserve a well-performing management team, and feedback is necessary in order to improve performance. If you institutionalize reviews, you are less likely to risk offending your board.

Reviews don't have to be lengthy, written affairs. They can be as simple as gathering feedback from you and the other directors and constructively delivering the results over coffee. For public company boards, formal reviews may be imposed by the institutional investors, but in a private company you don't need to make this complicated. Come up with simple criteria, like attendance, preparation, time spent between meetings, quality of discussion, value added to results, and so on, and apply them uniformly across your board. People will know what you expect and how they measure up.

As ventures evolve, they will most likely require different expertise and experience from the board. If board evaluations are performed regularly and effectively, everyone should be open to natural transitions. These events should not be taken personally. When recruiting board members, it is important for you to point out that their roles are likely to change over time; otherwise, changes down the road become awkward.

Your chief financial officer has a special relationship with your board.

S ome inexperienced board members may consider the CFO to be just a glorified accountant. The CFO and CEO are, however, the only officers in the venture with overarching fiduciary duties. The CFO has a duty to present accurate financial data, even if it is inconsistent with the CEO's narrative. The CFO has a duty to report transgressions, like human resource complaints, and opine on issues like the company's viability and its business outlook. Don't be mistaken: there is only one leader, and it is the CEO, but the CFO is more than just a member of the management team; she or he is also a fiduciary to the board.

As such, the board should have unfettered access to the CFO, even without the CEO being present. The CFO should also expect unfettered access to the board. This applies especially when the CFO is playing a larger strategic and operating role in the organization, such as managing legal affairs and human resources, which is often the case in early-stage companies.

Inexperienced and insecure CEOs may try to restrict the CFO's access to the board. Don't let that happen. The board should be sensitive to the politics but unwavering in their support of this special relationship. Direct access to the CFO helps to ensure some form of checks and balances in the venture. The CFO liaises with the audit committee, which can serve as a forum for presenting his or her view of the business, as well as an opportunity to raise any concerns directly with the board. The board should actively seek the CFO's views in meetings in order to encourage candor and avoid any awkwardness with the CEO. For good governance, you must respect this relationship and not interfere with the board's direct access to the CFO.

The founder should choose the best CEO available.

F ounders often have two very different roles in a venture. They provide the vision and commitment that only someone who has birthed the venture can bring. And, most often, they have a management role, frequently serving as CEO.

You should not be confused about the difference. Unless you have led a rapidly scaling startup and have experience building and managing an organization, developing product, driving sales and marketing, overseeing finances, and creating a profitable business, you are just an understudy CEO. The mythology that the founder should scale with their business all the way to operating a public company, as Bill Gates did at Microsoft, for instance, has its roots in a time when ventures grew more slowly. It was difficult but possible for a brilliant person like Gates to scale "just in time" with his business. Today it is still possible, but harder, and it calls for a different construct. Mark Zuckerberg did it at Facebook, but only with the experienced Sheryl Sandberg at his side, and Larry Page learned at the feet of Eric Schmidt and Bill Campbell before returning to the helm.

In the early stages of a venture, the most important elements are the founder's vision and innovativeness. The focus is on creating a product and building a small team;

there is no business to run yet. But as the business develops, operating skills grow in importance until they become paramount to success. The more successful your venture is, the more likely it is that you won't be able to keep up by learning on the job.

That is when founders need to be acutely aware of the two distinct roles they play. As the founder and a significant stakeholder, you owe it to your team and fellow stakeholders to provide them with the best leadership you can find. If you are not the right CEO, you should replace yourself. After all, what is more important: the success of your vision or your CEO title? It is much more valuable to be an excellent entrepreneur than a mediocre CEO; you can hire well-trained and experienced management.

It is a good practice to work with the board to outline their expectations of the CEO for each stage of the business. The job specification will change as the company develops. If you are clear on what you need to accomplish, you should be the first person to notice when you are falling behind. Don't wait for things to deteriorate to the point that your board has to step in. As the founder, you should actively solve the leadership gap by recruiting the best people, especially when you are hiring your own replacement.

The board may seek to coach a founder/CEO or find an outside professional to help the founder/CEO get beyond their limitations, but, as with couples' counseling, this often leads to divorce anyway. If the venture is showing signs of persistent poor management or inexperienced leadership, such as an exodus of talent or the inability to meet schedules and budgets, directors often are left with only one effective tool in their toolbox: replacing the founder/CEO.

Letting go of a founder/CEO is not without its challenges. The two biggest risks an investor ever takes are making their initial investment and replacing the founder. Founders bring vision, innovativeness, passion, and dedication that are almost impossible to replace. It is preferable that the founder stay engaged in some significant role. A common solution is to make the founder the chairperson of the board, to highlight their ongoing contribution and keep them fully motivated. It's even better if they can play an instrumental executive team role without undermining the new leader—you might make them the chief technology officer if they are a technology visionary, or chief strategist if they are adept at predicting trends and working with outside partners.

We had this very experience with a promising venture led by a passionate young entrepreneur. He was creative and tireless. But he was a mercurial leader. He fired his co-founder within months of starting the business, over some minor concerns. Then, one by one, he found fault with each member of his executive team. He continued to drive execution, but it was bogging down because of his obsessive micromanagement. Ultimately, some of his team approached the board in private and threatened to leave if things weren't resolved. The board brought in a human resources consultant to interview each of the team members and deliver the CEO an anonymous assessment of his performance, something referred to as a 360-degree review. He took it poorly, feeling wrongly persecuted. The board then made the difficult decision to replace the CEO rather than lose the team. He became the vice president of marketing. After reluctantly working with the board to recruit his replacement and being granted his personal choice of CEOs, the founder nevertheless quickly clashed with the new leadership. The board removed him from his operating role but left him as a director. When the going got tough, his obstreperousness almost sank the ship. It was a sad result. He was clearly the right entrepreneur but the wrong leader.

Early-stage companies are generally too small to have well-developed succession plans. Searches for new leadership take time, and there are no good job specifications for entrepreneurs. Finding an experienced operator who can successfully partner with a founder is difficult at best. There are interim CEOs who can stand in during an extended search, but they act as caretakers, not leaders, and the venture is likely to flounder in the meantime. During any transition, the directors, and the lead director in particular, need to prioritize the time to vet candidates, calm the organization, and provide guidance to the remaining team so they can stay on track. Ideally, boards should be constructed so that there is someone who can step into a crisis on a short-term basis. All too often, however, startups mistakenly believe that this is a luxury they cannot afford.

RULE 75

Find a coach.

You are on a steep learning curve. There are people's livelihoods and vast sums of money at stake. You can't afford to fail. Don't fake it. Find someone who can help you surmount the hurdles and push your limits, even if the ultimate result is your choosing your replacement.

There are various terms tossed around for this person: adviser, coach, mentor. They are not all the same.

An adviser brings missing experience and crucial expertise. They advise you on areas outside your own strengths and knowledge. They have a very tactical role, based upon their domain. They can be helpful when you are undertaking a new challenge or confronting an unfamiliar issue. Advisers make you a more knowledgeable CEO.

A coach is there to train you, to improve your skills. They help you become fit for the job. They might work with you on your overscheduled calendar or your communication style or your leadership of team meetings—whatever is holding you back at the moment. They bring a wealth of insight that can prepare you for the big event. Coaches make you a more skilled CEO.

Mentors are the rarest of the three. They are your life teachers. They don't necessarily bring any arcane domain knowledge. They aren't there to improve your skills per se.

They are there to make you better, period—to help you grow and develop as a person, as a leader, not just as a CEO. They invest in you personally, not necessarily in your venture. They are more interested in your character than your career. If they feel that your role, or your job, is not the right fit for your personal development, they will tell you. Mentors make you a better you.

Chemistry is important to all of these relationships, but your chemistry with a mentor is paramount. They have to buy into your potential and character and commit to telling you the unvarnished truth. And you have to commit to hearing it.

Many founder/CEOs have benefited from mentors. In Silicon Valley, Bill Campbell was revered for his mentorship. Sure, he could advise on sales and marketing and coach CEO skills, but it was his extremely rare talent for bringing out the best in others that made him a revered mentor. Steve Jobs, Larry Page, Eric Schmidt, Scott Cook, Jeff Bezos, and even one of us all enjoyed the warmth, friendship, and dedication of Bill Campbell.

So look for advisers who can make you smarter. Don't hesitate to find a coach who can improve your performance. And if you are very lucky, you may stumble upon a mentor who can make you great.

Not all things can be taught or learned, however. Whenever confronted with someone's limitations, Bill Campbell would famously say, "You can't coach height," meaning that, in the end, you either have it or you don't. When you confront your limits, do what is best for the company and find a great replacement.

It is the CEO's job to run efficient, productive meetings.

You have assembled a board of busy and influential people. They have numerous opportunities to invest their time and energies. Many have full-time jobs and their own problems to keep them occupied. You need to be cognizant of that in managing the board's time and activities.

Too many board meetings are dog and pony shows put on by management to entertain the board. They cover performance, financials, governance issues, and key metrics in minute detail.

The meeting is a rare occasion for you to engage your brain trust on the problems and decisions that keep you up at night. It is a time to bring them up to speed on critical information and changes since the last meeting and to give them context. Context is important for reviewing and debating the issues that are critical to your success. Plan ample time for the board to ask questions and discuss meaty issues. Don't make the meetings lectures or you will end up with bored and disengaged directors. Remember: your board comes from operational and investing backgrounds, and they enjoy chewing on difficult problems.

A board meeting is also a good moment for you to take a step back and think like an owner instead of just a manager lost in the daily grind; it is a time to see the forest and not just the trees. The preparation for the board meeting affords you a chance to contemplate your business through a wider lens. A board meeting, therefore, is a good moment for you and your board to get aligned around both strategy and tactics.

Even with an ideal five-member board and no observers, meeting a couple of hours a month and once each quarter for three hours, time is tight. For the benefit of argument, let's take a deeper look at the three-hour meeting once a quarter. Let's assume that a total of thirty of the 180 minutes are lost to warm-up discussions, breaks, and wrap-up. Let's further suppose that management presentations and reports take up three-quarters of the remaining time. That leaves slightly over thirty-five minutes for questions, discussion, debate, and decisions. If each significant issue takes an average of ten minutes of discussion, that leaves only enough time to discuss three and a half issues—with even less opportunity for questions or comments from each of the directors. That's hardly worth their time and attention. How efficiently you manage the board meeting is therefore critical to getting the most out of your board.

Think about turning the meeting on its head. Address company status, metrics, financials, and other reporting data in pre-meeting materials. Annotate and summarize well so the board can digest them without accompanying color commentary. Highlight critical insights so they sink in. Save the precious board-meeting time for big issues and hard questions where the board can add significant value. Whether in pre-meeting materials or at the meeting itself, never overwhelm the board with reams of data and appendices. It is your job to distill the information they need so as to get the most value from them. Focus on and prioritize the things that keep you and your team up at night.

Think of these discussions as breaking into two broad types: descriptive (What is going on? How are you performing with respect to plan?) and prescriptive (What key decisions do you need to make now to ensure that you are successful going forward?). Manage the schedule closely, but provide time for constructive digressions without threatening to crowd out other important topics. Unchecked meetings spend too much time on the descriptive and not enough on the prescriptive.

You can start by reviewing key takeaways and insights from the pre-meeting materials in the board meeting to make sure they register. But whatever you do, don't recite your slides to the board. And don't let your team do it, either. Nothing puts a board to sleep faster than reading aloud. Their eyes might be open, but their brains are turned off.

RULE 77

Don't "oversell" your board.

Y ou sold hard to land your funding and assemble your board. You sell every day to recruit employees, forge alliances with partners, tell your story to the press, and convince the world that you are onto something big. When you get to the board meeting, stop selling.

Your board is savvy to selling. They probably do it themselves, every day, for a living. But as your brain trust and confidants, they don't want to be sold by you. They want the straight scoop. They want to wrestle with the facts and overcome the challenges with you. If they are to be effective, they need to know the unvarnished truth. Don't sell the board.

You need to fully inform and engage the board. Arm them to be useful. If you use board meetings to sell your decisions, you are squandering the opportunity for your board to bring their best game to your business. Furthermore, you are likely creating skepticism that ultimately may erode your credibility. Nobody knows better when they are being sold than someone who sells for a living. There may come a time when you do not have the benefit of the doubt needed for a crucial vote if you have already wasted it by overselling.

Some less experienced CEOs or founders can fall into the trap of treating their boards with disdain or even contempt. You might hear them utter things like "They don't understand my business," "Board meetings are a waste of time," "I'm not going to discuss any bad news because the board always overreacts," and so on. If these comments sound familiar, then you only have yourself to blame. After all, it's your responsibility to ensure that the board is effective and productive. If they are not living up to your expectations, don't put them in a box and turn off the lights. Make it a board discussion, and get their input on how you can better manage them and your meetings.

If management is constantly selling its decisions rather than opening themselves up to question and discussion, the board loses perspective on the real issues and trade-offs, resulting not only in a breach of trust but also in suboptimal decision making. And it can make for surprises down the road as you course-correct, seemingly inexplicably, because the board did not fully understand the issues giving rise to your decision. How could they, with all the selling you've been doing to obscure your challenges?

That does not mean that you shouldn't emphasize and celebrate the good news. Board meetings should be balanced. It is good practice to start a board meeting with a slide of "Highlights" (things that went well) and a slide of "Lowlights" (things that disappointed). And for good measure, add a slide at the end of "Things That Keep Me Up at Night." That way, the board can sync up on the key issues and check in at the next board meeting on how those concerns are going.

And it doesn't mean you should prematurely share anxieties that are not yet ripe problems. Always declaring that the sky is falling is not the alternative to overselling. There is a comfortable place in between.

Make sure to fully inform the board so that you can solicit their help, opinions, and feedback. An uninformed board is useless. A smart board won't overreact to bad news and will be open to new ideas and strategies as things change.

RULE 78

Board agendas should look like this.

There is no universal agenda for a good board meeting. Each CEO and board should create their own format to suit their needs. But there are some best practices that can inform your agenda. Here is one approach for a three-hour board meeting.

1. **Introduction and Overview:** Highlights, Lowlights, and What We Hope to Accomplish Today. | 15 mins.

   Set the agenda and objectives for the meeting. This is also a good time to review "Things That Keep Me Up at Night" from the prior meeting.

2. **Performance Status Update**: What We Have Accomplished Since the Last Meeting. | 25 mins.

   Update the board on important insights from your key metrics, your financial performance since the last meeting and for the year to date, your engineering schedules, product status, etc. Include comparisons of current performance to the plan and earlier forecasts, complete with explanations. Follow up on any assignments from the last meeting.

3. **Forward-Looking Business Update.** | 25 mins.

Track alignment of your latest forecast with the annual operating plan, focusing on any adjustments and the reasons for them. Share new data and learnings that affect the plan. Discuss the future of your business, including your product road map, hiring plan, financing strategy, competition, sales forecasts, and proposed new initiatives, as well as any corrective efforts needed to get your venture back on plan if you are lagging in any regard.

4. **Break:** Check Emails and Phone Calls, Make Pit Stops. | 15 mins.

Enforce this religiously. If your directors know when to expect a break, they are less likely to pick up their phone or leave the room during the meeting. Include two breaks during the meeting if possible. You will have a better chance of keeping the board in the room and attentive. The quid pro quo is that they must return promptly so you can stay on schedule.

5. **In-Depth Discussions.** | 60 mins.
   i. Discuss the most pressing challenges you are facing (ideally no more than two or three). | 30–45 mins.
   ii. Discuss new opportunities for success. | 15–30 mins.

6. **Conclusions.** | 15 mins.

    i. Get alignment on all key decisions and the direction you propose to take.

    ii. Assign any board tasks and make any requests of the board for action before the next meeting.

7. **Closed-Door Session.** | 15 mins.

Ask your team to leave the room. It is customary for your CFO and, regarding corporate legal topics, your counsel to remain if they are relevant to the discussion, but when the topics are particularly sensitive to them, you may ask them to exit as well. Cover all corporate business and get board approvals for your employee stock options, board resolutions, and any other governance items.

8. **Private Session.** | 10 mins.

You leave the room. The outside board members discuss outstanding issues among themselves. Feedback is communicated back to you directly by the lead director.

RULE 79

Prepare thoroughly for board meetings.

Y ou should commit to sending out the board materials at least two business days in advance of the meeting, to afford directors time to read, digest, and consider the materials. While it's your responsibility to make sure the meeting time is used wisely, every director is responsible for reviewing the materials in advance. Too often, directors—particularly investors with large portfolios and numerous boards—open the materials for the first time at the meeting itself. Directors should prepare ahead of time any issues they would like to focus on or add to the board discussion and communicate them to the lead director or to you for consideration for the board agenda.

Consider providing each director with a hard copy of the materials at the board meeting so they don't have to bring theirs or refer to their computers or tablets. Written copies allow you to keep everyone on the same page and assure you that they are not attending to their email instead of giving the meeting their undivided attention.

Directors are advised to have available the materials from the prior meeting so they can compare as necessary. With the different decks laid out next to each other, it is easier to ensure that stories aren't changing, commitments aren't slipping, and critical items aren't being dropped. Even better, in the presentation materials you can report all performance information, like key performance indicators, objectives and key results, and financial reports, in the form of chronologically comparable rows of metrics, with your own commentary on what the trends and any deviations indicate.

It may sound minor, but there is a nomenclature issue here, and it is important to distinguish the following metrics. The annual operating plan (AOP) is prepared once per year and approved by the board at the start of the fiscal year. This is the official plan of record for the company. The AOP is then periodically updated in the form of forecasts, typically quarterly, that reflect changes to the AOP based upon your performance to date and any new information. While the forecast becomes the new plan of record, it is still important to track performance to the original AOP as well. Otherwise your ability to create accurate plans will not improve with experience. Being accountable for variances breeds mastery.

RULE 80

Use your daily management materials for board meetings.

For a venture losing money and burning cash, time is quite literally money. So your aim is to spend as little time as possible preparing quality board materials by using readily available management scorecards, presentations, key performance indicators, objectives and key results, etc. The materials you and your team review every day and report on at weekly management meetings contain the primary content for the board meeting. If they don't, you are doing something wrong.

The board wants to know how you and your team are performing and what challenges you are facing. Much of that should be in the materials your team is using in the normal course of business. Repurpose those same materials for the board, taking into account that they may need more explanation, elaboration, and context because your board is not thinking about your business every day.

Additionally, you can ask each team member to submit a couple of slides that highlight their performance and any challenges. If you have everyone work off the same template, you can easily assemble these reports into one coherent board package. Better yet, have your CFO or counsel take responsibility for harmonizing the presentation. In the end, you are responsible for what is in the presentation, so make sure to review it in detail and put your stamp on it before sending it out.

One common mistake is inundating your board with too much material and information. Remember: like you, these are busy people. And also like you, they expect communications to be crisp, short, and to the point. Don't distract your board with marginally helpful but unessential data. You can add other materials in an appendix for further reference, but even that may be overkill.

If you can short-cut the heavy lifting of preparing pre-meeting and presentation materials while focusing your board on only the most important information, you can then spend your collective attention working on the big issues. Board discussion time is one of your scarce resources—often less than twenty hours per year—so put your energies into that, not into making pretty slides.

_____

Too many unanimous board decisions is a sign of trouble.

If your board seems to always arrive at a unanimous consensus, no matter how difficult the question and regardless of how uncertain you are personally about the answer, then you may have a problem. It can signal three things: (1) there is too much groupthink, (2) your board is not challenging you enough, or (3) you are not communicating well as a board. Worse yet, maybe they are simply checked out.

Boards and CEOs often feel uncomfortable with split board decisions. This is likely the product of the lawyers: they like board minutes that reflect unanimous votes, because they believe such a record will stand up to challenge in the event of litigation. After all, if everyone agrees, it must be sound business judgment. But often it is quite the opposite.

Split decisions demonstrate that smart people are listening and thinking, independently. That is the type of board you want. The more genuine the discussions and debates, the better the understanding and trust among the various parties. Too many unanimous decisions may signal that your board is relinquishing its authority or is disempowered.

Sadly, it is not uncommon to see a history of unanimous board decisions followed by the firing of the CEO, seemingly out of the blue. Everyone was in agreement, and his reviews were fine, so what happened? What happened was that the board members were not truthfully communicating their concerns, and the CEO did not have the benefit of understanding their feedback. They were "getting along" rather than challenging one another. That is very troubling for all concerned.

It is important to encourage directors to speak up and ask tough questions. Don't pressure them to come to an agreement. A healthy board process benefits from differing opinions, and the questions and disagreements need to surface if you are going to have the opportunity to address them. It's your job to listen, consider, and then decide.

Following open debate and healthy disagreement, the entire board may support a single decision even if they would have preferred another, but this should be the result of a fully engaged deliberative process and not a rubber-stamp approval. Discussions and debates are different from voting. In the discussion, everyone's differing perspectives should be invited and aired. But the vote is not on whether you would personally prefer the suggested action, but rather whether, after full debate and deliberation, you can honestly support the decision. And it goes without saying that once a vote has been taken, it's important that everyone support the decision, regardless of their vote or personal opinion.

Use working sessions and committees to reinforce your priorities.

B etween board meetings, directors should be encouraged or required to participate in specific working sessions with you and your team. Working sessions force directors to acquaint themselves more deeply with the details of the venture. By including board members in those aspects of the management process where they can add value, you will increase the likelihood that decision making is done collectively, as a team rather than as a confederation of individuals. Working sessions also help directors appreciate the complexity of some of the day-to-day issues so they understand the difficult trade-offs you are facing. This is an opportunity for your team as well. They are able to demonstrate their abilities to the board and get to know them better, and in turn the board can better evaluate them.

Convening board subcommittees is helpful, because it sets a precedent for directors to participate in some but not all of the most pressing governance issues. For instance, those board members with financial expertise can serve on the audit committee, while other directors with more recruiting experience might serve on the compensation committee. This is especially important when the CEO might need to exclude certain board members from various discussions because of conflicts of interest—for example, when a significant investor is also a potential acquirer, vendor, or competitor of the venture.

Establishing a formal committee instead of just relying on a working session also signals to the rest of the organization the topic's level of importance. For example, ventures for which continually raising capital is critical to their long-term strategy might form a special strategic finance committee, and companies that are subject to strict regulatory oversight, such as online lending companies, might form a compliance committee.

———————

Your board should spend time with your team.

E xpose your best performers to your board. This can serve as encouragement for your team as well as a call to action, and it can reinforce performance accountability. If you want to enforce deadlines, asking the responsible person to present the issue at the next board meeting is a powerful motivator. Everyone wants to make a good impression with the board. You should guide them on how to present and communicate effectively so they use their exposure to maximum benefit.

These meetings also allow the team to hear directly from the board so they can appreciate the board's priorities and concerns. In return, it is a chance for the board to gain a deeper appreciation of the talent throughout the company and understand their capabilities, aspirations, and challenges. This will be helpful to you when you are recommending someone for a promotion or a raise. If the board already knows them and appreciates their work, your job just got easier.

Working sessions with your team are one way to facilitate this exposure. Another way is to arrange for Q&A sessions following board meetings or at specific predetermined events (e.g., quarterly all-hands meetings). This can be conducted with the entire company or with select groups. It is a useful way for board members to personally contribute to and evaluate the venture's culture and morale and to directly communicate their perspectives. This also sets the stage for more direct lines of communication if sensitive issues arise where employees feel the need to go around their management with concerns, like claims of sexual harassment or improper business practices. They should feel comfortable and welcome approaching board members with any problems they think are crucial for the company and unresolved by management.

Of course, all of this requires a great deal of trust in the sensitivity and skills of the board members. They must be resolute in not disrupting the organization, engendering politics, or exposing confidences.

And when employees do raise questions about the leadership, the board needs to react swiftly and deliberately. If the board doesn't, it will lose the trust and confidence of the organization.

PART 5

ACHIEVING LIQUIDITY

P art 4 presented rules for how to create an effective board and manage it well.

In part 5, we discuss the often misunderstood issue of liquidity, commonly confused with the much-touted "exit." There will come a time when you and your investors will want to unlock some of the value you have created. This is called achieving liquidity. Liquidity is not always an exit, an event by which an owner sells their entire stake in a company, but exits always entail liquidity. Public offerings are often seen as the pinnacle of cashing out, but mergers and acquisitions account for far more liquidity events. And short of an IPO or merger or acquisition, there are secondary markets, private equity investors, and even venture investors who can provide some liquidity when needed. The rules in this section will help you prepare for your various liquidity options.

Build companies to last, providing liquidity along the way.

B uilding something that lasts and achieving liquidity are not mutually exclusive. In a sort of mantra, investors often instruct their management teams to ignore any sale or liquidity event and just work diligently to create a sustainable business. It seems like the right thing to say.

Entrepreneurs certainly have the power to create engines for wealth, impact, and innovation. Too often, though, there is confusion about exactly what they are building. Inventors create new technologies. But a technology is not a product until it is made useful. And a product is not a company until you have assembled the organization to launch it in the marketplace. And a company is not a business until it can make a profit and sustain itself with the money paid by satisfied customers rather than begged from investors.

Growing a valuable, independent business should be the prime directive. While it's true that some spectacular outcomes do come to pass before a venture has a viable business or even a customer—think WhatsApp selling to Facebook for nearly $20 billion, without any visible means of support, or LuxVue, the breakthrough LED display company no one has ever heard of because it was bought by Apple before it ever delivered a single commercial screen—those are the rare exceptions. But building a business that makes more money than it spends and grows faster than its competition is the tried-and-true path toward creating value (and liquidity). Nothing else is within your control.

Nevertheless, when opportunity knocks, answer it. If you are onto something big, others will see it, too, and some may prefer acquiring you to competing. You may choose not to let the opportunity in, but at least open the door.

At some point in time, and certainly when institutional investors have provided you with capital, you will be looking for some liquidity event or events as you build your business. This is how venture capitalists return money to their limited investors—the pension funds, sovereign wealth funds, endowments, foundations, and individuals who provided their venture fund with the money they invested in your business. When you accept money from a venture capitalist, you are agreeing explicitly, in something called a "redemption clause," or implicitly to make their shares valuable and liquid at some point so they can handsomely repay their investors. Don't accept institutional capital if you are not committed to achieving liquidity, or insurmountable conflicts are bound to arise. And even if you don't have institutional investors, at some point your employees will want to taste the fruits of their labors.

While a liquidity event may be an exit for some investors who sell their ownership stakes and move on, it also offers a financing opportunity for your company. You need to have a strategy for how to reward your employees and investors that is consistent with your strategy to finance your continued growth. Liquidity is not necessarily the final outcome, but it can be a healthy step along the path toward building a successful business.

Liquidity is not limited to initial public offerings and acquisitions.

Liquidity is often associated with an IPO (initial public offering) or the sale of the company. There are, however, more options for you to consider, especially in a time when private ventures can amass stockpiles of money and stay private and independent for longer periods. It is important to understand the liquidity timing expectations of your various stakeholders in order to avoid conflicts and friction. The good news is that there are a variety of tools you can employ that will allow your stakeholders to benefit from one or more liquidity events while continuing to grow your venture.

Here are some of the tools available for achieving liquidity:

1. YOUR VENTURE CAN USE ITS OWN CASH TO BUY BACK STOCK FROM SHAREHOLDERS. That is assuming you have the money. Even though this approach is straightforward, it can raise concerns for your stakeholders if your venture does not have better uses for its cash than to purchase shares back from investors and employees. If you choose to buy back shares, it is important to manage the possibly negative signaling to the market and to make sure you are husbanding sufficient cash for ongoing growth and unforeseen risks. It would be very embarrassing, if not disastrous, if you used your bank account to buy back stock, only to hit a pothole in the business that forces you to scramble for more capital. In a private venture, determining the buy-back price is a challenge. And if you offer to buy back shares from some but not all of your stakeholders, you may encounter dissent and even litigation. With good counsel and perhaps bankers, this generally can be managed, but it is not simple.

2. INSIDE INVESTORS CAN BUY THE STOCK OF OTHER SHAREHOLDERS. This is loosely referred to as a secondary sale. A primary sale is when the company sells its shares and receives the proceeds. A secondary sale between private parties is when a shareholder in the company sells their shares and receives the proceeds. The company does not offer any new shares. This would result in some insiders increasing their ownership percentage while providing liquidity to others. (Note: There is also something called a secondary offering made by a company that has already conducted a primary offering through an IPO, where they issue new shares and directly receive the secondary proceeds. This is not what we are talking about here.)

The advantage of this approach is that there is no particular fundraising round or event to manage, no boring pitches to make, no legal fees or new investment terms. This is simply a transaction between private parties. The stock purchase agreement most likely provided the company with a right of first refusal to any shares sold in a private sale, and you (and any shareholders who may own a similar right) will have to waive it.

Once again, setting the private price can be tricky. But

whenever someone wants to sell, there is a buying opportunity for others, and this is an arm's-length deal. Note that you need to consider whether you are comfortable with increasing the buying investor's ownership stake and consequent clout in your business. You also need to be sure the pricing does not run afoul of any employee option pricing (discussed further below) or anticipated future fundraise.

3. SHAREHOLDERS CAN SELL STOCK INDIVIDUALLY AS PART OF A COMPANY-WIDE FUNDRAISE. This approach is a hybrid of the primary and secondary sales in which the company manages the process that creates the demand and gives some or all of existing shareholders the opportunity to sell some of their shares to the new investor as part of the primary sale. The advantage of this approach is that the company receives the proceeds of the primary sale, while the selling shareholders receive some liquidity in the secondary sale, allowing the new investors to acquire shares from both the company and preexisting owners, at the company's negotiated price. This is an elegant solution when new investors demand more ownership than the company is willing to sell in primary shares alone. A complication may occur if common shares are sold with preferred shares, since each needs to be valued separately, but there are accepted mechanisms for doing so.

Whenever your shareholders sell stock—back to the company or to someone else—there are some pitfalls to watch out for. The price is one. Common shares and options are priced more advantageously than preferred shares. The additional rights associated with preferred shares makes them more valuable. When the board grants employees options, the board has to establish a strike price, which is the price that the employees will eventually pay for the option when they exercise it and receive their stock. That price is most often the fair market price; otherwise in the United States the employee is deemed to have received compensation equal to the overage that is taxable immediately upon the grant. This is bad, because the options are not liquid, and the employees will have to reach into their pockets to pay the tax.

There are mechanisms for third-party experts to value private company common stock, resulting in what is termed a 409A price in the U.S. Barring material changes to the business, the board can rely on that valuation in setting the option strike price for one year. The sale of common shares, or even of the preferred shares upon which their value is based, at a price different from the company's recent pricing can derail your well-managed process, resulting in taxes for employees and an increase in the strike price for future options to employees. Increasing the strike price of future options makes them less attractive for the purposes of recruiting.

Furthermore, secondary sales will result in changes to your capitalization table. This can introduce new shareholders you would prefer not to have, like competitors. In the United States, if the list gets long enough, it may require you to register with the SEC and subject yourself to regulatory compliance prematurely. The original stock purchase agreement should be written to give you control of all secondary sales so you can decide these issues and not have them decided for you. To protect your company's interests, you need to be involved closely in any secondary sales.

4. YOU CAN CHOOSE TO GO PUBLIC, OR, MORE FOR-MALLY SAID, CONDUCT AN INITIAL PUBLIC OFFERING. The IPO process in the U.S. normally takes three to six months commonly with the assistance of investment bankers, and involves registering with an exchange in accordance with SEC regulations. This not only provides liquidity through the sale of your publicly traded stock but also raises funds for the company's growth. Going public is not inexpensive, however. It requires months of distractions for senior management: an exhausting road show where management repeatedly sells public investors on the merits of the business, significant legal and accounting costs, large investment banking fees if you use bankers, and ongoing stringent regulatory and reporting compliance that will change the way you do business. In the United States, if you qualify under the recent JOBS Act, the process becomes somewhat easier for small growth ventures but riskier for the investors.

5. YOU MAY CHOOSE AN OUTRIGHT SALE OF YOUR BUSINESS TO A THIRD PARTY, UPON WHICH ANOTHER COMPANY PURCHASES YOUR VENTURE EITHER WITH STOCK, CASH, OR A COMBINATION OF BOTH. Private equity firms may also be acquirers if you meet their criteria, which is usually an undervalued business with large positive cash flows. A sale is a clean way of achieving both liquidity and an exit, but it is rife with issues of integration, loss of control, and strategic direction.

A few clever companies have used a sale to slingshot their business by leveraging the assets of the acquirer, while others have disappeared into oblivion. Donna Dubinsky and

Jeff Hawkins were unable to raise all the capital needed to adequately launch their PalmPilot business. U.S. Robotics, a modem company with plenty of cash but poor prospects, approached them with an acquisition offer that promised them access to the full faith and credit of the parent and, most important, their money. With that, Donna and Jeff successfully launched not just a product but a new wave in portable assistants. They later spun off from their parent company and formed Handspring, the first real smartphone business. Of course, they are exceptional entrepreneurs; you may not want to try this at home.

RULE 86

If you go public, don't slip and fall.

The early venture capitalists were hardened operating executives, not glorified financial engineers. They would make sure the company's best years were ahead before offering stock to the public, because the ongoing success of the venture was imperative to them. Tom Perkins was proud that at Kleiner Perkins, the returns to limited partners who held shares in ventures that went public had been much greater than for those who sold in the IPO.

The actual public offering might be relatively small and at a seemingly low price but designed with a clear expectation that there will be subsequent secondary offerings as the company's value grows. Your venture then has the time to successfully develop an attractive public market for its shares, allowing the market to get to know your business and value your long-term performance and growth potential. This approach has successfully created enduring wealth for companies, their founders, their employees, and their investors.

Today, companies often remain private longer, partly in hopes of maximizing their IPO proceeds and price, but frequently resulting in missing the optimal pricing window or stumbling out of the blocks by failing to meet the high expectations the company has engendered. It's important to remember that your maximum value is a function of both the amount of your revenues and profits but also your growth rate. So waiting too long can actually lead to lower valuations, in spite of higher revenues and profit. For instance, if you have profits of $100 and an expected growth rate of 100 percent per year, you might be valued at $10,000. But if you have profits of $200 and an expected growth rate of 20 percent per year, you might be valued at $4,000. The retrenchment in the value of so many prominent unicorns (private companies with a valuation of $1 billion or more) as they approach liquidity is testimony to this problem.

Investors' and management's interests in liquidity often conflict.

Investors may argue against the sale of a venture below a certain price—even when it would provide a respectable outcome for all. They expect a larger multiple and return on their investment and are willing to roll the dice to get more. This is an easy argument for VCs to make, because they are maximizing the returns on their portfolio of bets rather than simply your venture.

To understand this point better, let's do some quick venture capital math. For ease of illustration, if a VC invests in ten early-stage startups, on average five will fail, three will return capital, and two will make most of the returns for the VC fund. Let's assume a minimum respectable return for a VC fund is 20 percent per year; this means a ten-year VC fund needs to return six times ($6\times$) its investment, net of fees, which are not insubstantial, in order to achieve the 20 percent hurdle. In order to accomplish this, the two winning investments each have to make a $30\times$ return to provide the overall venture capital fund with a 20 percent compounded return.

So while your sale to a strategic acquirer with a resulting $5\times$ return might be a good outcome for the company and its employees, the venture investors are likely to be conflicted.

This further underscores the importance of prequalifying all investors regarding their liquidity expectations, time frame, and fund status. All the stakeholders should appreciate that when a liquidity opportunity exceeds the risk-adjusted valuation, effectively receiving tomorrow's value today without the risk of execution, it may be a good time to sell. Smart investors who have been in the game for a while know that, while they may aspire to returns of 10× or more, markets and ventures are highly unpredictable, and a bird in hand may be worth it even if it's a tad skinny.

Individuals need liquidity, too.

Liquidity is an important strategic event for you and your board, and it starts by understanding the needs and expectations of all of your stakeholders. While events like initial public offerings or mergers and acquisitions may provide liquidity to your entire capitalization table of investors and employees, key individuals have their own personal needs for liquidity regardless of your financing strategy. A young founder who has been with the company for a while may be looking to buy a first home or might be expecting a child. If she or he is struggling with founder compensation issues and needs some cash, partial liquidity may offer a solution.

The benefits could be significant for the venture, because it alleviates stress and allows the individual to focus on the business—avoiding a potential retention issue down the line. Investors often feel that any form of early liquidity in which the investors do not participate should be avoided, in order to keep interests aligned and to eliminate any negative signaling to employees and future investors. How do you explain that your founder just sold $1 million of his stock when you are trying to convince a new employee that her options have infinite upside? Also, early liquidity for a few may exacerbate the problem of delaying liquidity for everyone else. Founders now worth millions are not as eager to pursue an IPO or acquisition as they were when they were only eating instant ramen.

The focus should be on their reasons for early liquidity and the size of their remaining incentives, including the percentage of ownership being sold, the percentage retained (do they still have enough motivation?), the mechanism for liquidity, and the price. You have to have a compelling message for employees and investors about why early liquidity for a few should not change their own enthusiasm for your business. If the need is great and the ongoing incentives still significant, you might be able to get past the lingering concern that these early sellers know something about the business that the rest of us don't.

There are secondary markets for these types of transactions, which simplify the process. Or it may be advantageous for everyone if a few employees sell some shares into an oversubscribed funding round to allow new investors with strict ownership requirements to buy more primary shares than the company is otherwise willing to sell. "No" may be the right answer to the question of early liquidity, but first ask the right questions and listen.

RULE 89

Your valuation will have a local maximum.

While most entrepreneurs and investors are loath to admit it, a venture is always for sale; it's simply a matter of price and terms. You hear heroic stories of entrepreneurs resisting large checks to go it alone and ultimately succeeding beyond their wildest dreams, like Mark Zuckerberg turning down Yahoo's $1 billion offer and building Facebook into a behemoth. What's missing are all the stories about the entrepreneurs and investors who turned down an attractive offer only to crash and burn. The latter cases are far more prevalent. The real question to ask when considering a sale is: Are the price and terms compelling in light of the risk ahead? The go-it-alone heroes may simply have assessed their risk of success differently, and more accurately, than their lowball suitors.

For most companies, however, there is an S curve in their valuation potential. As growth slows, the increase in the rate of valuation also slows. While many people may believe that the scale of revenues and profits are the most important drivers of company value, for ventures the growth rate can be even more important. This means that waiting for larger revenues and profits as growth rates slow further along the S curve could be highly counterproductive.

This is especially true for more capital-intensive business models. Once the technology has been proven, the return on capital to establish global sales, the supply chain, balance sheet strength, and so on is often not the best use of venture capital. Consider a biotech company whose small team has invented a breakthrough drug but now is confronted with the daunting expense and risk of having to build a large-scale manufacturing, distribution, and sales business. It might be time to transition the company's source of funds and balance sheet composition to a lower-cost capital structure. You may choose to bring on later-stage private equity investors whose economics are based on lower risks and lower returns or sell to an acquirer with a lower cost of capital.

Consequently, entrepreneurs and venture investors should always be mindful of their "local maximum." In mathematics, the concept known as maxima and minima refers to the largest and smallest values of a function. If those values are measured over a defined range—say, time—then they are referred to as the local maximum and local minimum.

The concept of local maximum has been adopted by business to refer to the highest value during a specific period of time or stage of the business. For instance, your business may have a local maximum value of $1 million before you demonstrate a product but a local maximum value of $5 million after you achieve $1 million in sales. You could say, "Well, $5 million is greater than $1 million, so I might as well wait before seeking liquidity." But if you consider the risks of developing the competencies to deliver a commercial product, sell it, and support the customers, plus the time and money it will take you to get there, it just might be smarter to accept an offer of $1 million, the pre-sales local maximum, instead.

Entrepreneurs tend to have a higher tolerance for risk and a greater appreciation for the many psychic rewards of ownership beyond the price, and venture investors who manage portfolios where the big winners pay for the many losers may also prefer rolling the dice rather than accept an early sale. Nevertheless, employees, individual investors, and later-stage investors have different appetites and may prefer to exit sooner than later. This potential conflict highlights your need to weigh the interests of all of your stakeholders in determining what to do about your local maximum.

A good rule of thumb is to never dismiss an acquisition offer out of hand, though you may well choose to reject it later. At the very least, it is good fodder for a substantive conversation about your local maximum value and the risk preferences of your investors and team.

Ventures aren't just bought; they can also be sold.

A successful sale requires an active, interested buyer. Yet placing a "for sale" sign on your business suggests a fire sale. Achieving an attractive sale of your company entails a methodical process to land the ideal, motivated buyer. Boards and investors often have little direct experience in the sales process and may believe that a favorable sale will only result from the initiative of an acquirer rather than through a disciplined effort by the seller. They toss around the adage that "companies are bought, not sold." But determining who is the predator and who is the prey is not always so easy.

A conventional investment banking process works well for selling companies with a substantial history of revenues, margins, profits, and cash flows, in a well-defined competitive landscape that potential buyers can analyze using a detailed information memorandum. Large strategic acquirers often hire bankers and deploy internal mergers-and-acquisitions teams to maintain a rolling database of established companies so they can better determine whether a strategic acquisition is attractive and whom to target.

Selling a startup venture rather than an established business, however, is more of a DIY effort. It is best conducted as an ongoing exercise with seven distinct steps, updated regularly to make sure you are ready when opportunity knocks.

Step 1: Map target acquirers.

Step 2: Identify influencers and decision makers.

Step 3: Determine key acquisition metrics.

Step 4: Study precedent transactions.

Step 5: Prepare materials.

Step 6: Connect.

Step 7: Be ready.

There is more discussion about each of these steps in the following chapters.

RULE 91

Choose an acquirer; don't wait to be chosen.

Identify the large, well-capitalized companies that are in your business or could benefit from being in it. There are many reasons they may be interested in acquiring you. They may need your product to satisfy their existing customers or to fend off their competition. They may need your team because they lack strong innovation. They may want your customers, either to add to their list or to prevent them from moving to their competitors.

They may have the infrastructure to be able to quickly scale your business without the growth or administrative costs you incur, resulting in an accretion of value for their company. Accretive value occurs when they can increase your profits by removing redundant costs while rapidly growing your revenues using the leverage of their existing business. One thing that makes accretive acquisitions particularly attractive is that the increase in the bottom line is immediately added to the acquirer's multiple of value. Shareholders are pleased.

An acquirer may also be interested in you personally, and in your vision. Innovative leadership is hard to come by, and larger companies are always on the lookout for entrepreneurs who can become intrapreneurs in their organization. Strategic acquisitions strengthen the legacy company's leadership bench and give them the chance to expand their business in new directions in order to fend off smaller, more innovative competitors.

After identifying potential acquirers, the next step is to rank them in their industries. You want to identify whether they are the industry leader, the hungry competitor, the new entrant, and so on. You need to understand the nature of the competitive juices that drive their decisions. The CEO of a number-three-ranked industry player may need some outside stimulus to move their company to a leading position and to be more highly valued by the public markets, while a number-one player may not. A number-three player may be more interested in a strategic acquisition, while the number-one player may be looking for an accretive acquisition. Consequently, a number-three player might be willing to pay a greater premium for an early-stage venture and be more likely to close quickly. On the other hand, if the number-one player perceives that its competition is threatening it with better innovation, it may be willing to pay more for a great creative team and leading-edge technology to defend its position.

The ideal scenario is to initially engage the most aggressive competitors and then approach the industry leaders to see if they are interested in defending themselves by acquiring you first. If you have only one interested buyer, you are doing all the selling, but if you have two or more, they are doing the buying. What you want is a bidding war.

Take the example of Graphiq, a big-data analytics company located in Santa Barbara, California. It was founded by Kevin O'Connor, a sharp and talented serial entrepreneur.

Kevin had a series of successes, including DoubleClick, which was ultimately sold to Google for $3.1 billion. Kevin's thesis for Graphiq was to focus on the valuable nexus of product information and purchase decisions—that is, to give users better and more information about products and services at the precise moment they are ready to make that decision. He also felt that, while big data and algorithms were necessary, they weren't sufficient. Graphiq used human editors to close the relevance gap with the customer struggling with a decision. The company evolved from a consumer comparison site to a service providing illustrative content to publishers. The business grew steadily, but not fast enough for Kevin's tastes. So in 2016 he decided to explore a possible sale of the company.

He hired an investment banker to help map out potential acquirers. They started by looking at the publishing industry. There were a handful of forward-thinking leaders in the industry, and Graphiq had relationships with many of them. But most of the targets were struggling with their own challenges in the declining publishing business, and none of them were comfortable enough with technology to bet big on a strategy that favored machine learning over their existing model.

So Graphiq recast its research. Graphiq's core assets were a big-data, machine-learning algorithm, the knowledge graph produced through these methods, and a brilliant team who could advance it. It just so happened that in 2016, the war between Google Assistant (number one) and Amazon's Alexa (number two) in the area of voice-driven intelligent assistants was heating up and spilling over to the likes of

Apple, Microsoft, and Samsung, among others. These were big, aggressive, technology-savvy players, duking it out in a huge and valuable market. In this battle, Graphiq had identified a much more promising set of potential acquirers who might be interested in their technology and their team.

This example makes clear why you should consider your list of targets a living document, and update it regularly as your venture and the market evolve. Don't limit yourself to the obvious targets, especially given how quickly markets change. That's what the acquirers are doing, and you, as a potential target of their interest, should be ready if and when they strike.

RULE 92

If you want to sell your business, you need to know the decision makers.

Each acquirer has its own internal process and one or more decision makers for buying companies. If you hope to get the acquirer's attention, you need to know these people and how they make decisions. Who are their board members, management team, M&A team, external advisers, bankers, and attorneys? All of these people are likely to have input into the process. You are probably just a couple of degrees of separation from one or more of these influencers through your own directors, advisers, and investors. After all, this is one of the reasons you chose these people for your ecosystem. Call on them to make the necessary introductions and to put in a good word when you are ready, so you can establish the right contacts when the time comes.

Second, map each candidate's internal decision-making process. How do they identify potential acquisitions? Who is charged with establishing these relationships? How do they qualify opportunities, and what is their process for evaluating businesses for acquisition? Who are the gatekeepers? Who actually makes the final decision? How long does this process take?

Talk to people who have sold their companies to the

acquirer, or who have been through the process and not sold their companies. Talk to the professionals who may have represented the acquirer or one of its acquirees, such as attorneys, investment bankers, and accountants, as well as any former employees who have experience with the process.

We strongly suggest that, whenever possible, you conduct these meetings personally. This information can be sensitive, and you want to create personal relationships that encourage people to be forthcoming. An added benefit is that each time you inquire, you also have an opportunity to position your company and spread the word. At the right time, this groundswell will be helpful in getting the attention of the acquirer.

But for the moment, this entire fact-finding-and-mapping process is done without ever speaking to the potential acquirer directly. All the information you need is generally available public market information, and the outside contacts can be identified without raising too much attention. Start casually rather than formally. Formal inquiries of the acquirer may start the clock and raise difficult questions you aren't prepared for or don't want to answer yet.

Back to Graphiq. After deciding that they were interested in potentially joining forces with Amazon, Google, Apple, Microsoft, or Samsung, Graphiq's leaders needed to find the best way into conversations with these targets. They had relationships with each of the American companies, but through their publishing business, not their big-data business. So they had to establish new contacts. Their existing contacts were helpful in identifying the decision makers within their organizations and were willing to put in a good word at the right time. The board helped identify the right top-level decision makers. Graphiq's bankers added their contacts to the list and shared their recent experiences with each of the acquirers so Kevin and his team could understand how each approached their acquisition decisions. His attorneys provided recent war stories and contacts to the effort. Graphiq knew who the decision makers were and the acquisition process for each of them. Now they were ready for the next step.

---

*Determine whether you are a good fit for an acquirer
before contacting them.*

Y ou need to know what the acquirer looks for in an
acquisition. This may seem like mind reading, but it isn't.
Carefully read all their analyst reports, earning transcripts,
press releases and interviews, and conference presentations.
They will discuss the attributes of any acquisitions they have
made in the past and often also report on their success. And
this can help you identify additional people for your due
diligence on the acquirers.

Furthermore, the reports lay out the narrative that the
acquirer is telling to investors and analysts so you can
understand where they think their business is headed and how
they should be valued. Pull together your own relevant facts
and metrics and compare them with what you know about
the acquirer's priorities. Ask yourself how the acquirer might
accelerate or improve their business if they were to acquire
yours. If you don't yet measure up, ask yourself what you need
to accomplish to be a good fit for the acquirer. This should
inform your execution strategy and timeline.

Before Graphiq could determine how they could make
a difference for each of the acquirers, they needed to
understand each company's strategy and approach to big-data

analytics. Amazon had recently made pronouncements about the success and importance of its Alexa business. Not to be outdone, Google was right on its heels and investing heavily in Google Assistant and its home products to compete with Alexa. Apple had Siri but was still forming its strategy for the home and had not declared its intentions yet, though it was clear to observers that Apple was already working on similar efforts. And Samsung was playing catch-up. There were press releases and analyst reports detailing each target's intelligent-assistant strategies. Interestingly for Graphiq, big-data and machine-learning businesses were rapidly becoming artificial intelligence darlings. Graphiq understood from its research that these giants were all aggressively confronting the challenges of voice-driven intelligent assistants in the home. Kevin now had the vital information he needed about how each company might benefit from what Graphiq had to offer.

You must understand what is in it for them before you worry about what is in it for you.

RULE 94

Know your acquirer's acquisition history in detail.

While the past is not an absolute predictor of the future, it will provide valuable information about the acquirer and its general approach to acquisitions. Research historical acquisition prices for past transactions by the acquirer and also by its competitors. These are your comparable transactions ("comps") and they will give you an idea about how your company might be valued. Review the information to determine at what stage your company needs to be in order to be valuable. Pay special attention to any business justification the acquirer may have given to investors or analysts for past acquisitions. Does this narrative apply to your business? Also determine how successful the acquisition was in the eyes of analysts and industry watchers. What strategic value did they receive in the transaction? Was the venture successfully integrated into the acquirer or left to languish? For instance, did the management team of the acquired company stay on and become integral, or did they leave quickly to pursue other things? These details are telling, because an acquirer that has been rewarded for successful past acquisitions is more likely to be aggressive in finding more.

You should present your findings to your board. They will help you qualify the candidates. Your board is likely to be most interested in your potential valuation. Reviewing the historical data will serve to align expectations. If you are at the wrong stage or in the wrong market cycle, or if the target acquirers are unlikely to pay what you think you are worth, it's good to know this sooner than later. Strategic acquirers may have a glass ceiling for valuing an acquisition, especially for ventures that do not have a long track record or proven, sustainable EBITDA (earnings before interest, taxes, depreciation, and amortization) or free cash flows. A lot of acquirers won't purchase any business that is not immediately accretive to their valuation. Even if you decide not to pursue an acquisition right now, you will be better off for having the data and openly discussing the options.

Graphiq relied on its bankers and its board to provide unpublished, nonconfidential information about the acquisition histories of each of its targets. Here is where your hard work finding the right investors and creating the best board pays off. Kleiner Perkins had special insights through its interactions with each of the targets on a host of other topics. The bankers, whom Kleiner introduced to Graphiq, had detailed information about market transactions. Other board members contributed their knowledge as well. Combining public information about transactions and the private-industry insights, Graphiq had a very good understanding of how each of the acquirers might value them. The comps took shape. Graphiq also had good information about how successful each target was in retaining and motivating talent after an acquisition. The ranking of the preferred acquirers was becoming clear.

RULE 95

Make yourself visible.

Nobody is going to buy you if they don't know who you are. You have to be a little coy to maximize your opportunity, unless you are desperate, in which case do whatever works.

It is best if the acquirer hears about you from others. Work with your marketing or PR people to get some attention in the press. Talk to analysts. Explain your business and your view of the industry. Become their sounding board and back channel. Be included in their articles and reports. Decision makers often make a habit of poring through industry press and analyst reports to track important developments.

Show up at conferences, or, better yet, present at conferences that you know the acquirer attends. Establish yourself as a thought leader with articles and interviews. Publish white papers about your technology and products. Your ecosystem can talk you up and recommend you to others. The goal is to build buzz and get everyone's attention.

A word of warning, however: don't package yourself just for the occasion or lose your authenticity. Some people are natural extroverts; others are more introverted. Do what comes naturally to you; just do more of it. If you like the limelight, get on stage or in the headlines. If you like thought leadership, publish or commune with the analysts. You don't want to be seen as mugging for the camera or stalking. But this is a good time to ratchet up your visibility in order to see if anyone notices.

Graphiq had always kept a low profile. Kevin was not one to pander to the press. The industry respected his company for its work, not its image. But it was time to get some attention. Graphiq reached out to analysts to explain its technology and vision. Kevin's team contacted the trade press to discuss their growth and success. And they did something quite ingenious: they produced a video. They found a way to legally hack into Alexa, for starters, and filmed their engineers querying the service while employing the Graphiq knowledge graph rather than Amazon's. The results were stunning. It seemed as if Alexa had gained a hundred IQ points. Kleiner Perkins had a long-standing relationship with Amazon and at Graphiq's behest shared the video with them. Amazon was impressed. Kleiner also had strong ties with Google and was intimately familiar with the leaders of Samsung, including the vice chairman. Additionally, Kleiner's business development team had a close connection with Apple's business development team as the result of a couple of recent transactions. And Kleiner's contacts at Microsoft reached all the way to Bill Gates. Graphiq was now able to use these connections to get attention inside the target acquirers.

Build a relationship with potential acquirers; don't cold-call.

Now is the moment to develop and prepare your promotional materials. This includes simple back-of-the-envelope business cases that can be discussed in casual meetings with the various representatives of the acquirer. These are intended to whet appetites, not to convince them to buy you. It's not a pitch per se. It may be a simple one-page introduction, or a sales package you use to describe yourself to your customers, or a few slides that highlight your most impressive metrics. Approaching target acquirers as potential customers or partners allows you to sell them on your value without ever suggesting that you are willing to sell your company.

Now that you are fully prepared, reach out and connect with the acquirer's decision makers. Meet them for coffee, or ask stakeholders to organize a lunch or dinner where the representatives of the acquirer are present. "Bump" into them at trade events. Make sure that they get to know you and your venture and are able to appreciate its strategic value so they will eagerly follow your progress.

Use these encounters to listen as much as to sell. As you gain understanding more directly from the acquirer about how they think about your business and their approach to acquisitions, you can refine your initial insights from your research into their acquisition history. In this way you will be able to qualify them better and, if you proceed, to tailor future discussion more specifically to their interests.

Follow up with emails and materials reporting your progress. Ask how you might work together, and listen closely to their answers. An effective means for building business relationships is to ask what you can do for them. But make sure you do it. If you make yourself useful, you will stay on their radar. Just meeting the decision makers is not enough; you want to make a favorable impression and form a relationship so you can continue the dialogue.

Armed with introductions from its board and bankers, Graphiq started knocking on doors. They used their own contacts elsewhere in the target organizations to sing their praises to the decision makers. They jumped on planes and visited the acquirers, equipped with an informational presentation and materials explaining who they were and where they were going. They assumed that the targets knew nothing about the capabilities of their knowledge graph. Strikingly, after all the research and preparation, their story was not about consumer decision making, publishing, or even big data; it centered on their knowledge graph and artificial intelligence. It discussed their technology and know-how, but in particular it emphasized their talent and leadership. They didn't start the meetings suggesting an acquisition; they talked about partnership, collaboration, and even the possibility of investment. But they very consciously kicked the acquisition door open.

Be ready when they are.

Anticipate and be ready when it's time to cross the line into bona fide acquisition discussions. If you have done your job well and been methodical about the process, the acquirer should be calling you.

There is a natural pace and rhythm to acquisition discussions. If you've tried your best to get an acquirer's attention for months without success, you may never get there. But if you feel that they are beginning to initiate the interactions as much as you are, then there is a basis for moving more deliberately.

As mentioned before, there is usually a local maximum for any exit valuation, both in terms of your venture's stage of development and the outside perception of your potential. You may think your business is not yet strong enough for a successful acquisition. But it is not uncommon for a venture whose business is sputtering to find that competitive changes in the market make them an attractive acquisition because of their technology and their team, not their revenues or customers. You may have created more option value than financial value. Regardless, value is value.

The ideal time to sell your venture is when your perceived

strategic and/or financial value is at its peak and all your stakeholders have had time to consider the alternatives and are in favor of a transaction. That is why you need to fully prepare and bring your board and investors through the process with you. You don't want to have to educate them at the last minute and rush their decisions if an offer comes in. Your stakeholders don't speak with one voice, and each will have their own considerations to wrestle with. Give them time to digest and come around to your thinking.

Having an active discussion among you, your team, and the board in managing this exploration exercise is important, even when the company is not formally for sale. This process, if done well, does not preclude your venture from going it alone—it just readies you to maximize the opportunity for a possible liquidity event when the moment is right.

It was time for Graphiq to drive to the close. The process had been ongoing for seven months now. There was interest from all the likely acquirers. Kevin had kept the board well informed of the discussions with the targets, the relevant comps, and the various alternatives, and the board was fully supportive of moving forward. The bankers served as point for the discussions with each of the targets. Kleiner Perkins provided the back channel for communications with the acquirers, to make sure nothing was lost in translation. Graphiq was now spending inordinate amounts of time meeting with the decision makers and hosting due diligence teams and operating managers at its headquarters (which, by the way, was just up the hill from a beach where you might find the

Graphiq team riding waves on days with good swells). Kevin's deep experience made him particularly sensitive to not creating high expectations at the company, expectations that might be dashed and that he would have to personally lead them back from.

Each of the acquirers processed the opportunity differently. And as the bankers herded them to a date for final offers, the targets started to diverge. When one of the targets lobbed in a lowball offer, Graphiq let the other acquirers know without disclosing any of the details. They were resolute in not sharing any specifics, because they did not want to be seen as shopping the deal and thereby risk losing the group's precious trust. But they did make their expectations clear by engaging in a "buy it now" rather than "at auction" strategy. When it was certain that the train was leaving the station, the negotiations became serious. Graphiq continued to be transparent about their expectations, and as each acquirer in turn tried to win the deal, Graphiq let them know that unless one of them hit their asking price, they were going to go to auction and evaluate their options afterward. They left the unmistakable impression that if the financial terms weren't rich enough, they might not sell at all.

Finally, in an eleventh-hour, late-night discussion, one of the acquirers bit the bullet and hit Graphiq's ante. It just so happened that it was Graphiq's first choice: Amazon. To make a long, ten-month saga short, after a spirited negotiation of the definitive agreement and a swift close, Graphiq is now a very happy and productive group inside Amazon, focused on making Alexa number one in the category and contributing to other parts of Amazon's organization with their expertise in artificial intelligence and machine learning. A happy ending, and a new beginning.

Success is not linear.

I t is a hard fight for every inch, every day. All successful ventures have gone through their fair share of ups and downs, including some that have faced the specter of bankruptcy before becoming well-respected, publicly traded stars. Consider Tesla's near-death experience in 2008. Moments after Elon Musk's startup looked into the abyss and saw its last dollar, Daimler invested $50 million, making it possible for Tesla to revive and unleash the imaginations of investors and customers alike. And let's not forget Apple begging Microsoft for a loan to keep the lights on just after Jobs returned in 1997. We know how well that turned out.

And then there is Twitter, Jack Dorsey and Evan Williams's phoenix that rose from their failed podcasting startup, Odeo. Max Levchin and Peter Thiel first conceived of PayPal as Confinity, a security company, before pivoting to payments. And Google was a pedestrian provider of search services to Internet portals like Netscape before necessity bred the invention of paid ads on the Google search results, and the rest is history.

Despite the uncertainties and the many challenges, you can beat the odds. Master the fundamentals, such as creating two business plans, leading a jazz band of game-changing executives, and managing like a maniac. Identify your leap-of-faith assumptions and discover your business by measuring what is important while carefully refining your path along the way. Scale your venture only as you remove risk and accomplish key milestones. Be frugal. Hire only the best, and be sure to keep them happy. Methodically develop your idea into a product, your product into a market, and your market into a business. Select the right investors. Be smart about how you raise your money. Build a good board and manage it well. And find the best opportunities for liquidity.

If you don't attend to the basics, you are just throwing the dice. If you lose discipline, chances are you will hit the rocks before reaching open water. Bad boards can sink a company as quickly as bad products. And the wrong investors may mutiny at precisely the wrong time. Be informed, prepared, and forewarned.

Maintain control of what you can control (i.e., all the above), and intelligently navigate the hazards to maximize your chances of success and to minimize your pain along the way. When you know what is going on in the heads of your investors and your board, you are better able to work with them. Sometimes smart people just do dumb things, but sometimes smart people do things that look dumb to you but make perfect sense if you know where they are coming from.

When setbacks do occur—and they will—remember that the journey is never linear, and every entrepreneur has been there before.

You are not alone.

RULE 99

Prepare for your lucky break.

Louis Pasteur famously said, "Fortune favors the prepared mind." For the entrepreneur, there is no more profound bit of advice. You may think you control your destiny, especially if you have been kissed by fortune in the past and take credit for the result. But experience attests to the fact that all the brilliance and hard work in the world will not matter without something happening that is outside of your control. To find a self-made man, you need a very narrow field of view.

Take the great Steve Jobs. He bought Pixar from George Lucas in 1986. It was a high-end computer system for rendering digital images. The business had limited success, and Jobs steered Pixar to the personal computer and ultimately to the software package RenderMan. But the company continued to struggle. Strategically, Pixar had created a small animation group, under the direction of a little-known computer animator named John Lasseter, to create demos showcasing its technology. As Pixar's prospects darkened, Lasseter started producing computer-animated commercials for customers to help keep the lights on.

It just so happened that Pixar also had a business relationship with Disney. Jeffrey Katzenberg was chairman of Walt Disney Studios and was responsible for the resurgence of its animated feature division, with such hits as *The Little Mermaid* and *Beauty and the Beast*. He had the idea of creating a CGI-animated feature film and tried to recruit Lasseter to direct it. Ironically, Lasseter had been fired by Disney years earlier, which lead to his working for Pixar in the first place.

Here is where Jobs was blessed by luck. Rather than join Disney, Lasseter convinced Katzenberg that he should retain Pixar to produce Disney's computer-animated features. Pixar signed a modest $26 million, three-film deal with Disney. Katzenberg was happy with this arrangement, because there was little precedent for a production company creating significant independent value. He must have figured he was giving himself the option to get a sweet price on Pixar at a later date. In the meantime, Jobs continued to try to sell the bleeding Pixar to Microsoft, but without success.

Toy Story was Pixar's first film, and it grossed a whopping $373 million worldwide. The first five Pixar films together grossed $2.5 billion. It was an unheard-of phenomenon, culminating in Disney's purchase of Pixar for $7.4 billion in 2006. Jobs did not pull the rabbit out of his own hat, but he was completely prepared for it when it appeared.

And let's not move on from Jobs just yet. After being pushed out of Apple in 1985, he founded NeXT, to make computer workstations for education and business. But it floundered. As with Pixar, Jobs tried to sell it with little success. In 1996, Apple was looking for a new operating system. It was in discussions to purchase Be Inc., a company founded by Jean-Louis Gassée, the former vice president of engineering at Apple, for a rumored $200 million. But Gassée was holding out for more than Apple wanted to pay. Apple balked, and in that instant Jobs's luck changed. He let Apple know that it could purchase the much more valuable NeXT for the bargain price of $429 million. Jobs joined Apple as a consultant, but he eventually returned as CEO to lead Apple to unprecedented innovation and financial success. Once again, it was not Jobs who created the opportunity with Apple; it was Gassée. But when luck changed, Jobs jumped on it.

This is not to take anything away from Jobs. He was a product and marketing genius. But history would look very different today if Lasseter had joined Disney or if Gassée had taken Apple's offer. The iconic Jobs may have been a footnote. Jobs could not create his own luck, but when luck turned his way, he had the people and strategy to take full advantage of it.

Jobs's frenemy Bill Gates was no stranger to good luck, either. In 1980, Microsoft was the leader in programming languages, like BASIC, for the PC cottage industry. When IBM decided to enter the PC market, it approached Gates and his co-founder, Paul Allen, about licensing Microsoft's languages for the IBM PC. At the meeting, IBM asked Gates about the best operating system for the project. Gates referred them to Gary Kildall at Digital Research, the owners of CP/M, the leading OS for the scruffy sandlot of PCs available at the time. Gates personally made the phone call connecting Kildall and IBM.

When IBM visited Digital Research, Kildall was absent. According to some reports, he was flying his plane, while others suggested he was on a business trip to the Bay Area. The IBM team presented Dorothy McEwen, his wife, with a typically one-sided nondisclosure agreement as a precursor to licensing discussions. McEwen refused to sign the agreement, and the IBM team walked away.

That was all the luck Gates needed. IBM contacted him about alternative operating systems. Gates knew of one at a small PC hardware company called Seattle Computer Products (SCP), which had developed QDOS for the newest Intel processor. Gates called SCP's owner, Rod Brock, and immediately licensed QDOS for $10,000 plus an additional fee for each company that Microsoft sublicensed. Steve Ballmer, Gates's lieutenant, told IBM about QDOS and asked if they wanted to buy it, but IBM passed, because they wanted the IBM PC to be an open platform. More good fortune for Gates.

IBM ended up paying Microsoft $430,000, including $45,000 for the Microsoft OS, which would eventually be called DOS. IBM expected to pay much more, but Gates wisely chose the right to sell DOS to other companies instead. The next summer, Gates bought QDOS outright for $50,000, and the rest is Microsoft.

Gates could not have arranged for Kildall to be absent, or for McEwen to balk at signing the NDA. But when the right circumstances presented themselves, he wasted no time buying up the alternative OS and partnering with IBM to sell DOS to the PC-clone industry. He was fully prepared for his lucky break.

And then there is Google. Early on, the company benefited richly from its own luck—in this case, bad luck. Larry Page and Sergey Brin's first business model was to provide their search engine to other Internet portals like Netscape. The portals monetized their own customers and sent Google a small fee. But their bad luck was that the portals were unable to monetize the rapidly soaring number of search impressions. Google was losing money and needed a better business.

Page and Brin considered placing banner advertising on the search pages but hated the user experience. Another company, called GoTo.com (later Overture), sold placements to advertisers wanting to be prioritized in their search results. The problem was that users saw search results ranked by how much advertisers paid, rather than according to their relevance to the user. Google tweaked the idea and placed the algorithmically relevant results on the left side of the page and the paid search results on the right. What ultimately became AdWords was a huge success, born of the bad luck that Page and Brin faced when the portals could not keep up with their search engine's overwhelming inventory. But Google would not have succeeded had it not been fully prepared with the team and technology to provide the best organic search results to capture the lion's share of search engine users.

Fortune does favor the prepared mind. And the corollary is also true: a prepared mind will not succeed without a little good fortune. Being brilliant just doesn't depend on being able to make it rain; it means being prepared with buckets to capture the unexpected downpour. It is a powerful skill to be able to seize the moment when your luck has changed. Professional gamblers are connoisseurs of luck and make a living by keenly determining when their fortune turns so as to increase the size of their bets. Be excellent—not because it is sufficient, but because it is *necessary* for success. To be a generator of success you also need to be a lightning rod for luck. We aren't talking about waiting for blind luck; we are talking about managing your luck. Sure, sometimes a house of money will fall out of the sky and land on an unsuspecting person's head, but that is no way to run a business.

RULE 100

Learn the rules by heart so you know when to break them.

Apprentices work furiously to learn the rules; journeymen proudly perfect the rules; but masters forget the rules. So it's been since the Middle Ages, and venture capital and entrepreneurship are no different. The venture capital world is minting more and more apprentices, while the masters, like Tom Perkins, are few and far between.

The rules in this book are battle-tested. Acquainting yourself with them will help you spot issues before they arise. Intuition is not just fast thinking from the gut; it is good judgment informed by knowledge.

Most rules are made for the average situation; they are meant to be broken when circumstances require. Our rules are no different. Let these rules serve as touchstones to guide your own difficult decisions along the way, not millstones to bog you down. Only you can decide which rules to apply, bend, or ignore as you face your own novel problems and opportunities.

You may well find a rule or two that you adamantly disagree with. If we have encouraged you to examine your own experience and arrive at a considered but contradictory conclusion, then we have done our job. Just don't mistake an exceptional event for a guiding principle.

We are seldom able to achieve exactly what we want in business. *Compromise* is not a dirty word. But you will do better in the end if you acquaint yourself with what others have done before. You know best, so be fearless, trust your intuition, and make your own rules once you've mastered these.

EPILOGUE: THE CARDINAL RULE

There are plenty of reasons to love entrepreneurship. Entrepreneurs live the creative life. They pursue their passions and challenge the status quo. They invent the future, on their terms, and can amass wealth and power in the process. They don't live lives of quiet desperation working nine to five for "the man" in soulless, dreary mausoleums. They have a sense of independence. And with all the surrounding celebrity comes importance.

Stodgy old companies try the equivalent of donning skinny jeans and coloring their hair by offering open floor plans and foosball tables to attract talent, but many young people prefer to carry a business card proclaiming them the CEO and founder of a fledgling spark of an idea, even if it means sharing a tiny ten-foot-square cubicle with their three other co-founders in a building warehousing scores of similarly hopeful independent thinkers. And before there are free lunches, there are always energy bars or, even better, that tasty food substitute Soylent.

From the outside, starting a company looks easy. Just wake up with an idea, tell your friends, and convince one or two people to partner up; take your pick of top-tier venture capital investors, build a product, get swarmed by offers, and sell to the highest bidder.

But we know it isn't really like that.

While wannabe entrepreneurs can quickly learn from a plethora of books, videos, podcasts, blogs, and tweets how to ideate, create a business plan, present, and hopefully raise some seed money, the rest is a bit more nuanced. How exactly do you execute on your plan? What is the best way to lead a team? How do you choose the right people? What distinguishes the best investors, and who are the right ones for me? How do you raise the proper amount of money to truly build a company? What is a board of directors, and why do I need one? How do you manage them? And then what about an exit? Is there a difference between an exit and liquidity, and which do I prefer? These vital questions are followed by a thousand more, about how to first take an idea and create a product, and then take a product and build a company, and then transform that company into a successful business.

You don't just dream up a company; you sweat the details and manage operations. You watch every nickel and are strategic about whom you raise it from. You lead through good times and bad. You assemble trusted advisers, coaches, and boards to keep you on track. You don't dream it; you work it—*hard*.

The headlong rush into the startup world can obscure the most important questions. Which brings us to our favorite rule. The one we love so much we buried it at the end, for all of you with enough commitment to entrepreneurship to arrive at this very spot.

THE CARDINAL RULE: ALWAYS ASK *WHY?*

Why this? Why you? Why now?

It's remarkable how often these questions stump entrepreneurs. After a long pause, they may respond with their vision, or a recitation of their mission, or just a simple "Because it will make a lot of money." But these aren't the answers we are looking for.

We want to know what makes you tick. We want to know why you care, and hopefully why we should as well. And we want to know why, among all the other opportunities and challenges we face at this very moment, your opportunity is important and ripe for success.

Don't prepare for these questions only because you suspect someone may surprise you with them; answer them because they are fundamental to your choice of the entrepreneurial life. With an ever-growing Mount Rushmore of billionaire prodigies, we need to be sure that "Why?" is answered clearly.

Financial success brings power, and power begets either privilege or responsibility. You choose. The world does not need more privileged entrepreneurs, or venture capitalists for that matter. We believe that if there is any meaning in success, it is about fulfilling your responsibility to others. To make a difference, not just a dollar.

Know *why* this venture is important to you. *Why* it should be important to others. And, given the low probability of success for any venture, *why* it is nevertheless worth failing at. Of course you don't want to fail; success is always preferable to failure. But if you fail, will you feel you wasted your time, or that you fought the good fight?

A great entrepreneur needs to be bright. And tenacious. And passionate. But great entrepreneurs must also have something to prove. Something to rebel against. Some greater calling to fulfill.

We hope this book expands your appreciation for what it takes to be truly successful. And if we did our job, these rules will accelerate and amplify your chances of beating the odds. Then you can create new rules to add to these first one hundred, and share them freely with others, as Tom Perkins did with us and with a generation of earlier entrepreneurs.

But most of all, we hope that our readers will use their success to create value, not just valuations. It's easy to lose your humanity if your success makes you feel superior to everyone else.

There is joy in mastery and pride in excellence. There is satisfaction in success. But there is true meaning and fulfillment in creating value for others and helping them reach their potential. In the end, successful entrepreneurship is the triumph of human potential.

A sage friend of mine who was a billionaire for a week or so during the 1990s tech bubble once told me that if you can have anything you want, then nothing has value. You don't have to make any choices. And if nothing has value, then neither do you.

We hope that these rules will help you to make a difference. In your business, in your community, and in your life. If you have the entrepreneurial gift, the gift of creation, then use it to make things better for everyone. And pay it forward by helping the next person fully achieve their potential and share the spoils with the world.

Keep yourself grounded and your wits about you by frequently asking yourself, *Why?* Entrepreneurship is important because it has the power to make the world better. That is *why* it is worth all the blood, sweat, and tears.

ACKNOWLEDGMENTS

FROM RANDY

This book would never have happened without Jantoon. It has been a wonderfully rewarding collaboration, and throughout the process, my admiration and respect for him have only continued to soar. Debra Dunn, my lovely wife, contributed her keen insights and uncanny edits. Her encouragement and advice made this book more than I could have envisioned. It was such a great pleasure to reunite with my editor, Hollis Heimbouch. Her mastery and friendship never fail me. She is the best. My friends and colleagues Eric Keller, Greg Woock, and Levi King provided invaluable early feedback that gave us reason to believe this book was worth the effort. My teammates at Kleiner Perkins, in particular my longtime compatriots Beth Seidenberg, Ted Schlein, John Doerr, Bing Gordon, and Brook Byers, have generously provided me with volumes throughout the years. Erin Lens, my trusty sidekick, always keeps me on track. The remarkable entrepreneurs and executives I have had the privilege to work with have taught me many secrets about life and business. And to Lola and Rufus, who have lain by my feet, day in and day out. They still don't know what I do, but they love me for it just the same.

FROM JANTOON

No words can describe my gratitude to Randy. I am as humbled as I am proud to have you as a mentor. I can never thank you enough for all the time, energy, and effort you continue to invest in me to make me a better human being. You are an awesome writer and the best partner in crime. My mentor and dear friend Tom Perkins, whom I miss dearly: your insights, intelligence, and raw honesty continue to guide me every day. My wise and beautiful wife, Sonia: you keep me grounded through all my crazy endeavors. My wonderful kids, Eric, Olivia, and Max, all of whom I love more than anything. To Hollis Heimbouch for understanding us so well. To Walter Presz Jr., Mike Werle, and Lars Andersen for teaching me to be a real operator. I would not be the person I am without your blind confidence in me. To my dear friends Michael Linse and Gaurav Bhandari for continuing to help me make sense of the world around me. To Sean Moriarty, a true leader and a contrarian, for your continued trust in me. And, obviously, to my fellows in the Stand, for keeping me honest.

ABOUT THE AUTHORS

RANDY KOMISAR is a venture capitalist with decades of start-up experience. He is the author of the bestselling book *The Monk and the Riddle*, about the heart and soul of entrepreneurship, as well as numerous articles on leadership and innovation. He is also the co-author of *Getting to Plan B*, on managing innovation, and *I F**king Love That Company*, on building consumer brands. He taught entrepreneurship at Stanford University and is a frequent lecturer at universities, as well as a regular keynote speaker on entrepreneurship, innovation, and leadership. He joined Kleiner Perkins Caufield & Byers in 2005 to focus on early-stage ventures. Prior to that he created the role of "Virtual CEO" to partner with entrepreneurs to help them and their businesses achieve their potential, serving as Virtual CEO for such startups as WebTV and GlobalGiving. He was a co-founder of Claris Corp. and served as CEO for LucasArts Entertainment and Crystal Dynamics. Randy was a founding director of TiVo and Nest. He was CFO of GO Corp. and Senior Counsel for Apple, following a private practice in technology law. He has also served on dozens of private and public company boards and advises such organizations as Roadtrip Nation and the Orrick Women's Leadership Board.

JANTOON REIGERSMAN is a seasoned financial operator with extensive experience in startups and growth companies. He serves as Chief Financial Officer of the publicly traded Leaf Group (NYSE: LFGR), a diversified consumer Internet company.

Earlier in his career, he served as CFO of Ogin Inc., as investor and member of Goldman Sachs' European Special Situations Group, and as investment banker at Morgan Stanley in its mergers and acquisitions team. He also initiated and led the 9000METER expedition, the first expedition to attempt 9000 vertical meters on human power by diving more than 152 meters below sea level and by climbing the summit of Mount Everest at 8,848 meters. He is a Fellow of the inaugural class of the Finance Leaders Fellowship and a member of the Aspen Global Leadership Network.